A Devotional Companion

Blessings and Prayers for College Students

BLESSINGS
&
PRAYERS

A Devotional Companion

for College Students

CONCORDIA PUBLISHING HOUSE · SAINT LOUIS

Foreword

The familiar words and rhythms selected for this devotional companion are drawn from the words often heard in worship as we gather in the community of Christ's church. The goal of this book is not to replace your Bible or hymnal, but to draw out from them various selections that speak to your life as a student. At the heart of this work are the Daily Prayer Offices for Morning, Noon, Evening and Close of Day. Following these are the texts from hymns, Scripture and prayers that can be used to complete the meditation. With this book you will be prepared to worship whenever your busy schedule permits.

I wish to express my appreciation to all those who are serving college and university students in our Synod. It is a challenging ministry and also a joyful ministry. Their love for the students whom they serve and their faithful service was deeply encouraging to all of us who worked on this book.

It is our hope that what has been drawn together in this little volume will aid you in coming before the Lord in every time and every circumstance and draw you more deeply into the church's primary texts for worship: the Scriptures and the liturgy.

Scot A. Kinnaman
Editor

Let the words of my mouth and
the meditation of my heart
be acceptable in Your sight,
O LORD, my Rock and my Redeemer.
Psalm 19:14

Contents

Prayer: The Voice of Faith [3]

Prayer does not begin in the human heart but in the hearing of God's gracious words of life and salvation spoken to us in the Gospel of His Son. Thus Luther explained the introductory words of the "Our Father" saying, "With these words God tenderly invites us to believe that He is our true Father and that we are His true children, so that with all boldness and confidence we may ask Him as dear children ask their dear father."[4] Just as faith comes by the hearing of Christ's words so prayer is created and sustained by the Word of the Lord.

The confidence is not in the praying heart but in the promises of God. In his classic little study of prayer, Dietrich Bonhoeffer wrote, "The richness of the Word of God ought to determine our prayer, not the poverty of our heart."[5] The human heart, that cesspool of sin and unbelief, is hardly the fountain from which the aroma of sweet-smelling prayer arises. Indeed the prophet Jeremiah said, "The heart is deceitful above all things, and is desperately wicked; who can know it?" (Jeremiah 17:9). Christian prayer is not based on the instincts of the heart, instincts that by their very nature rob us of the fear, love, and trust in God above all things. Instead, our Lord invites us to pray in His name, that is, on the basis of good and gracious will and His sure promises.

Oftentimes prayer is described as a conversation with God. This is a helpful image if we keep in mind that God always has the first word. We can speak to God in prayer only because God has first spoken to us in His Son. We are reminded of this blessed reality in the prayer offices of Matins and Vespers as the versicle from Psalm 51:15, "O Lord, open my lips, and my mouth shall show forth Your praise," is chanted. It is only as God opens lips locked by sin that mouths are free for the full-throated prayer that delights the ears of our heavenly Father. When we sinners try to open our own lips in prayer, we know what happens. Instead of praise and thanksgiving, intercession and supplication, out come petitions of self-justification and attempts to bargain with God. Prayer then becomes a tool of unbelief that is used in a vain and self-serving attempt to pry from the hands of God the answer that we want rather than the gifts that our Father would give us. When prayer becomes unglued from the Word of God, it is transformed into a weapon that sinners would use against God in a foolish attempt to have their own will done on earth.

Prayer is not an instrument that we use to get something from God. To use the language of Lutheran theology, prayer is not a means of grace.

God richly and lavishly bestows the forgiveness of sins, life, and salvation on sinners for the sake of the atoning death of Jesus Christ. Our Lord wills to give us these gifts in the concrete and earthly instruments that He has designed and established for His church. In Baptism, God washes away our sin and gives us the gift of His name and Spirit. The words of absolution unchain us from the fetters of our sin by the power of Jesus' death. In the Lord's Supper we feast on the fruits of the New Testament given in the body and blood of the Lamb of God. This means that when we are troubled and tortured by our sin and the hellish attacks of Satan, we do not take comfort in the strength or sincerity of our praying but in the rock-solid gifts won for us on Jesus' cross and delivered to us in the means of grace.

C.F.W. Walther noted the spiritual damage that is done when sinners are directed to their own prayers rather than the Gospel: ". . .the Word of God is not rightly divided when sinners who have been struck down and terrified by the Law are directed, not to the Word and the Sacraments, but to their own prayers and wrestling with God in order that they may win their way into a state of grace; in other words, when they are told to keep on praying and struggling until they feel that God has received them into grace".[6] Our confidence is not to be found in our prayers but in God's work in Word and Sacrament. Pietism, both in its classical and contemporary forms, directs troubled consciences to prayer and thus burdens them with the law. The fruit of faith rather than faith's source becomes the focus and struggling sinners are set up either for despair or pride.

When Law and Gospel are properly divided, prayer will be seen as anchored in and fueled by the Gospel. To use the words of Eugene Peterson, "prayer is responding speech."[7] That is, the Christian speaks to God in prayer because he or she has first listened to the Holy Trinity in His Word. The Sacred Scriptures, the Catechism, and the liturgy tutor us in such praying.

Adolph Koeberle wrote, "Prayer escapes the danger of disorder and confusion only when it is enkindled by the words of Scripture. From the Word proceeds its inner justification, as well as its life-giving power and the clearness of its petitions. A prayer that does not stick to Scripture will soon become poor in ideas, poor in faith, poor in love, and will finally die."[8] Martin Luther recognized how prayer is "responding speech" in the advice on prayer that he gave to his barber, Peter. Luther encouraged Peter to tie his prayers to the text of

> As human beings learn to talk by listening to others around them, so liturgical prayer must be learned by listening to "Our Father," to the Word addressed to us, and to the company of the family of God among whom we live. Where that lively and life-giving Word is received in the heart of faith, the prayer that is 'conversation with God' happens.
>
> – Kenneth Korby[1]

Scripture, taking a text like one of the commandments and turning the text into a prayer*. In this way prayer is anchored in the Word of God and not allowed to become the playpen of human emotion and imagination.

Thus the Catechism became the prayer book for Luther and the Lutheran church. Not only did the Catechism provide splendid instruction in prayer shaped by the Gospel as we can see from Luther's treatment of the "Our Father," the Catechism also provided some very basic forms for prayer set within the rhythm of daily life (morning and evening prayer, prayer at meals). Moreover, the Catechism itself could be prayed!

The liturgy also becomes a tutorial in Christian prayer as the liturgy not only gives us the words and gifts of the Triune God, but also gives us God's own words so we might faithfully confess His gifts, extol His saving name, and call upon Him in prayer and intercession. Prayer shaped by the liturgy draws us out of our inborn selfishness, freeing us to use prayer in faith toward Christ and in love for the neighbor. As the liturgy is first and foremost, *Gottesdienst* (divine service) or God's service to us, liturgical prayer reminds us that prayer is always a response to what God says and does. Hearing God's words, we use His words to speak to Him.

---

*See "A Simple Way to Pray," *Luther's Works*, American Edition, Vol. 43, pp.193-211.

God has given His children a wonderful privilege in prayer. Prayer is abused if it is reduced to a spiritual technique for acquiring blessings from a stingy deity. The God who has given us His Son tenderly invites us to trust His Word and call upon His name with boldness and confidence.

> The richness of the Word of God ought to determine our prayer, not the poverty of our heart.
> – Dietrich Bonhoeffer[2]

Daily Prayer for Individuals and Small Groups

These brief services are intended as a simple form of daily prayer for individuals, families, small groups, and other settings.

When more than one person is present, the versicles and responses may be spoken responsively, with one person reading the words in regular type and the others responding with the words in bold type. Prayers may be prayed in the same fashion, though those in bold type are to be prayed by all.

For the readings, several verses have been recommended for each particular time of day. These may be used on a rotating basis. The value in using these few texts lies in the opportunity to learn them well. For those desiring a more complete selection of readings, daily lectionaries, such as those found in a hymnal, may be used. Meditations as well as readings from Luther's Small and Large Catechisms may be included.

In the "prayers for others and ourselves," the following suggestions are intended to establish a pattern of daily and weekly prayer.

Sunday: For the joy of the resurrection among us; for the fruit of faith nourished by the Word and the Sacraments.

Monday: For faith to live in the promises of Holy Baptism; for one's calling and daily work; for the unemployed; for the salvation and well-being of our neighbors; for schools, colleges, and seminaries; for good government and for peace.

Tuesday: For deliverance against temptation and evil; for the addicted and despairing, the tortured and oppressed; for those struggling with sin.

Wednesday: For marriage and family, that husbands and wives, parents and children live in ordered harmony according to the Word of God; for parents who must raise children alone; for those looking for a faithful spouse; for our communities and neighborhoods.

Thursday: For the Church and her pastors; for teachers, deacons and deaconesses, for missionaries, and for all who serve the Church; for fruitful and salutary use of the blessed Sacrament of Christ's body and blood.

Friday: For the preaching of the holy cross of our Lord Jesus Christ and for the spread of His knowledge throughout the whole world; for the persecuted and oppressed; for the sick and dying.

Saturday: For faithfulness to the end; for the renewal of those who are withering in the faith or have fallen away; for receptive hearts and minds to God's Word on the Lord's Day; for pastors and people as they prepare to administer and receive Christ's holy gifts.

The sign of the cross may be made by all in remembrance of their Baptism.

In the name of the Father and of the ✠ Son and of the Holy Spirit. **Amen.**

O Lord, in the morning You hear my voice;
in the morning I prepare a sacrifice for You and watch. *Psalm 5:3*

My mouth is filled with Your praise,
and with Your glory all the day. *Psalm 71:8*

O Lord, open my lips,
and my mouth will declare Your praise.
Psalm 51:15

Glory be to the Father and to the Son and to the Holy Spirit; as it was in the beginning, is now, and will be forever. Amen.

A hymn, canticle, or psalm may be sung or spoken.

An appointed reading or one of the following is read: *Colossians 3:1–4; Exodus 15:1–11; Isaiah 12:1–6; Matthew 20:1–16; Mark 13:32–36; Luke 24:1–8; John 21:4–14; Ephesians 4:17–24; Romans 6:1–4.*

A meditation or selection from the catechism may be read.

The Apostles' Creed is confessed.

Lord's Prayer

Prayers for others and ourselves

Concluding prayers:

Almighty God, merciful Father, who created and completed all things, on this day when the work of our calling begins anew, we implore You to create its beginning, direct its continuance, and bless its end, that our doings may be preserved from sin, our life sanctified, and our work this day be well pleasing to You; through Jesus Christ, our Lord. Amen.

I thank You, my heavenly Father, through Jesus Christ, Your dear Son, that You have kept me this night from all harm and danger; and I pray that You would keep me this day also from sin and every evil, that all my doings and life may please You. For into Your hands I commend myself, my body and soul, and all things. Let Your holy angel be with me, that the evil foe may have no power over me. Amen. (Luther's Morning Prayer, Small Catechism)

Let us bless the Lord.
Thanks be to God.
Then go joyfully to your work.

The sign of the cross may be made by all in remembrance of their Baptism.

In the name of the Father and of the ✠ Son and of the Holy Spirit. **Amen.**

Listen to my prayer, O God, do not ignore my plea;
hear my prayer and answer me.
Evening, morning, and noon
I cry out in distress and He hears my voice.
Cast your cares on the Lord and He will sustain you;
He will never let the righteous fall.
Psalm 55:1, 16–17, 22

Glory be to the Father and to the Son and to the Holy Spirit; as it was in the beginning, is now, and will be forever. Amen.

A hymn, canticle, or psalm may be sung or said.

An appointed reading or one of the following is read: *1 Corinthians 7:17a, 23–24; Luke 23:44–46; Matthew 5:13–16; Matthew 13:1–9, 18–23; Mark 13:23–27; John 15:1–9; Romans 7:18–25; Romans 12:1–2; 1 Peter 1:3–9.*

O Lord,
have mercy upon us.
O Christ,
have mercy upon us.
O Lord,
have mercy upon us.

Lord's Prayer

**Prayers for others
   and ourselves**

Concluding prayers:

Blessed Lord Jesus Christ, at this hour You hung upon the cross, stretching out Your loving arms to embrace the world in Your death. Grant that all people of the earth may look to You and see their salvation; for your mercy's sake we pray. **Amen.**

(OR)

Heavenly Father, send Your Holy Spirit into our hearts, to direct and rule us according to Your will, to comfort us in all our afflictions, to defend us from all error, and to lead us into all truth; through Jesus Christ, our Lord. **Amen.**

Let us bless the Lord.
Thanks be to God.

The sign of the cross may be made by all in remembrance of their Baptism.

In the name of the Father and of the ☩ Son and of the Holy Spirit. **Amen.**

A candle may be lighted.
Let my prayer rise before You as incense;
the lifting up of my hands as the evening sacrifice. *Psalm 141:2*

Joyous light of glory of the immortal Father; heavenly, holy, blessed Jesus Christ. We have come to the setting of the sun, and we look to the evening light. We sing to God, the Father, Son, and Holy Spirit: You are worthy of being praised with pure voices forever. O Son of God, O giver of life: the universe proclaims Your glory.

A hymn, canticle, or psalm may be sung or said.

An appointed reading or one of the following is read: *Luke 24:28–31; Exodus 16:11–21,31; Isaiah 25:6–9; Matthew 14:15–21; Matthew 27:57–60; Luke 14:15–24; John 6:25–35; John 10:7–18; Ephesians 6:10–18.*

A meditation or selection from the catechism may be read.

Lord's Prayer

Prayers for others and ourselves

Concluding prayers:

Lord Jesus, stay with us, for the evening is at hand and the day is past. Be our constant companion on the way, kindle our hearts, and awaken hope among us, that we may recognize You as You are revealed in the Scriptures and in the Breaking of the Bread. Grant this for Your name's sake. **Amen.**

Let us bless the Lord.
Thanks be to God.

Mealtime Prayers:

Asking a blessing before the meal

Lord God, heavenly Father, bless us and these Your gifts which we receive from Your bountiful goodness, through Jesus Christ, our Lord. Amen.

Returning thanks after the meal

We thank You, Lord God, heavenly Father, for all Your benefits, through Jesus Christ, our Lord, who lives and reigns with You forever and ever. Amen.

The sign of the cross may be made by all in remembrance of their Baptism.

In the name of the Father and of the ✠ Son and of the Holy Spirit. **Amen.**

The Lord Almighty grant us a quiet night and peace at the last.
Amen.
It is good to give thanks to the Lord,
to sing praise to Your name, O Most High;
To herald Your love in the morning,
Your truth at the close of the day.

An appointed reading or one of the following is read: *Matthew 11:28–30; Micah 7:18–20; Matthew 18:15–35; Matthew 25:1–13; Luke 11:1–13; Luke 12:13–34; Romans 8:31–39; 2 Corinthians 4:16–18; Revelation 21:22–22:5.*

The Apostles' Creed is confessed.
Lord, now You let Your servant go in peace; Your word has been fulfilled. My own eyes have seen the salvation which You have prepared in the sight of every people: a light to lighten the nations and the glory of Your people Israel. *Luke 2:29–32*

Glory be to the Father and to the Son and to the Holy Spirit; as it was in the beginning, is now, and will be forever. Amen.

Lord's Prayer

Prayers for others and ourselves

Concluding prayers:

> The sea of this world lies between where we are going, even though we have already seen where we are going. And what has God done? He has provided the wood by which we may cross the sea. For no one can cross the sea of this world unless carried by the cross of Christ.
> — Augustine[9]

Visit our dwellings, O Lord, and in Your great mercy defend us from all perils and dangers of this night; for the love of Your only Son, our Savior Jesus Christ. Amen.

I thank You, my heavenly Father, through Jesus Christ, Your dear Son, that You have graciously kept me this day; and I pray that You would forgive me all my sins where I have done wrong, and graciously keep me this night. For into Your hands I commend myself, my body and soul, and all things. Let Your holy angel be with me, that the evil foe may have no power over me. Amen. *(Luther's Evening Prayer, Small Catechism)*

Let us bless the Lord.
Thanks be to God.
Then be at peace and rest in God's care.

What's in a Name?

O LORD, our Lord, how majestic is Your name in all the earth! You have set Your glory above the heavens.

No student can begin, continue, or complete a college education without being exposed to dozens of famous names in the arts and sciences. Renoir, Dostoevski, Shakespeare, Einstein, Kant—on and on they go. Most names represent greatness and a kind of "intellectual immortality." Names represent famous people past and present.

There is another name that is above all names. It represents more than a famous historical person. It is the Lord! How majestic is Your name, O Lord, Your glory is above the heavens! This majesty and glory is owned and shared by Jesus Christ, our Lord and Savior.

This name represents Him in whom we trust for new life, spiritual renewal, and salvation. To believe in His name does not mean to give a cold mental assent to the history and facts of what Jesus did. It is rather to rest all our cares and fears, sins and anxieties, on Him—as Savior and Helper. It is to believe in Christ and what He did for us in His death and resurrection. It is He who has given us forgiveness of sins and a new life of fellowship with God.

What's in a name? In His name we share the glory of being God's own. It is to confess with the famed poet-preacher John Donne that "Caesar is not Caesar still, nor Alexander Alexander, but Jesus is Jesus still and shall be forever." We represent our Lord's name to others and demonstrate its uniqueness among all the hosts of great mortal men and women who still must bow before the Lord of lords and King of kings. Let us firmly resolve to keep His name in the limelight of life. May this glorious name never be dimmed by the lesser lights of His creatures.[12]

Christians, while on earth
   abiding
Let us never cease to pray,
Firmly in the Lord confiding
As our parents in their day.
Be the children's voices raised
To the God their parents
   praised.
May his blessing, failing never,
Rest upon his people ever.

Bless us, Father, and protect us
From all harm in all our ways;
Patiently, O Lord, direct us
Safely through these fleeting
   days.
Let your face upon us shine,
Fill us with your peace divine.
Praise the Father, Son, and
   Spirit!
Praise him, all who life inherit!
   (*LW* 434)

Text: Johan Olaf Wallin

Every service is a structure of acts and words through which we receive a sacrament, or repent, or supplicate, or adore. And it enables us to do these things best—if you like, it "works" best—when, through long familiarity, we don't have to think about it. As long as you notice, and have to count, the steps, you are not yet dancing but only learning to dance. A good shoe is a shoe you don't notice. Good reading becomes possible when you need not consciously think about eyes, or light, or print, or spelling. The perfect church service would be one we were almost unaware of; our attention would have been on God.

—C. S. Lewis[19]

Selection of Hymns

—Used elsewhere in this book—

A Mighty Fortress Is Our God

1. A mighty fortress is our
     God,
   A trusty shield and weapon;
   He helps us free from every
     need
   That hath us now over
     taken.
   The old evil foe
   Now means deadly woe
   Deep guile and great might
   Are his dread arms in fight;
   On earth is not his equal.

2. With might of ours can
     naught be done,
   Soon were our loss
     effected;
   But for us fights the valiant
     One,
   Whom God himself elected.
   Ask ye, Who is this?
   Jesus Christ it is,
   Of Sabaoth Lord,
   And there's none other
     God;
   He holds the field forever.

3. Though devils all the world
     should fill,
   All eager to devour us,
   We tremble not, we fear no
     ill,
   They shall not overpower us.
   This world's prince may still
   Scowl fierce as he will,
   He can harm us none,
   He's judged; the deed is
     done
   One little word can fell him.

4. The Word they still shall let
     remain
   Nor any thanks have for it;
   He's by our side upon the
     plain
   With his good gifts and
     Spirit.
   And take they our life,
   Goods, fame, child, and wife,
   Though these all be gone,
   Our victory has been won;
   The Kingdom ours
     remaineth. (*LW* 298)

Text: Martin Luther

All Praise to Thee, My God, This Night

1. All praise to thee, my God, this night
For all the blessings of the light.
Keep me, oh, keep me, King of kings,
Beneath thine own almighty wings.

2. Forgive me, Lord, for thy dear Son,
The ill that I this day have done;
That with the world, myself, and thee,
I, ere I sleep, at peace may be.

3. Teach me to live that I may dread
The grave as little as my bed.
Teach me to die that so I may
Rise glorious at the awesome day.

4. Oh, may my soul in thee repose,
And may sweet sleep mine eyelids close,
Sleep that shall me more vigorous make
To serve my God when I awake!

5. When in the night I sleepless lie,
My soul with heavenly thoughts supply;
Let no ill dreams disturb my rest,
No powers of darkness me molest.

6. Praise God, from whom all blessings flow,
Praise him, all creatures here below;
Praise him above, ye heavenly host;
Praise Father, Son, and Holy Ghost. (*LW* 484)

Text: Thomas Ken

All Christians Who Have Been Baptized

1. All Christians who have been baptized,
   Who know the God of heaven,
   And in whose daily life is prized
   The name of Christ once given;
   Consider now what God has done,
   The gifts He gives to ev'ryone
   Baptized into Christ Jesus.

2. You were before your day of birth,
   Indeed from your conception,
   Condemned and lost with all the earth,
   None good, without exception
   For like our parents' flesh and blood,
   Turned inward from the highest good,
   You constantly denied Him.

3. But all of that was washed away—
   Immersed and drowned forever
   The water of your Baptism day
   Restored again whatever
   Old Adam and his sin destroyed
   And all our sinful selves employed
   According to our nature.

4. In Baptism we now put on Christ—
   Our sin is fully covered
   With all that He once sacrificed
   And freely for us suffered.
   For here the flood of His own blood
   Now makes us holy, right and goodness
   Before our heav'nly Father.

5. O Christian, firmly hold this gift
   And give God thanks forever!
   It gives the power to uplift
   In all that you endeavor.
   When nothing else revives your soul,
   Your Baptism stands and makes you whole
   And then in death completes you.

6. So use it well! You are made new—
   In Christ a new creation!
   As faithful Christians, live and do
   Within your own vocation,
   Until that day when you possess
   His glorious robe of righteousness
   Bestowed on you forever! (JV)

Text: Paul Gerhardt
Tune: Nunfreut euch

Baptized into Your Name Most Holy

1. Baptized into your name
   most holy,
   O Father, Son, and Holy
   Ghost,
   I claim a place, though weak
   and lowly,
   Among your seed, your
   chosen host.
   Buried with Christ and dead
   to sin,
   I have your Spirit now
   within.

2. My loving Father, here you
   take me
   Henceforth to be your child
   and heir;
   My faithful Savior, here you
   make me
   The fruit of all your sorrows
   share;
   O Holy Ghost, you comfort
   me
   Though threatening clouds
   around I see.

3. O faithful God, you never
   fail me;
   Your cov'nant surely will
   abide.
   Let not eternal death assail
   me
   Should I transgress it on my
   side!
   Have mercy when I come
   defiled;
   Forgive, lift up, restore your
   child.

4. All that I am and love most
   dearly,
   Receive it all, O Lord, from
   me.
   Oh, let me make my vows
   sincerely,
   And help me your own
   child to be!
   Let nothing that I am or
   own
   Serve any will but yours
   alone. (*LW* 224)

Text: Johann J. Rambach

Chief of Sinners Though I Be

1. Chief of sinners though I be,
   Jesus shed his blood for me,
   Died that I might live on high,
   Lives that I might never die.
   As the branch is to the vine,
   I am his, and he is mine.

2. Oh, the height of Jesus' love,
   Higher than the heavens above,
   Deeper than the depths of sea,
   Lasting as eternity!
   Love that found me wondrous thought
   Found me when I sought him not.

3. Only Jesus can impart
   Balm to heal the wounded heart,
   Peace that flows from sin forgiven,
   Joy that lifts the soul to heaven,
   Faith and hope to walk with God
   In the way that Enoch trod.

4. Chief of sinners though I be,
   Christ is all in all to me;
   All my wants to him are known,
   All my sorrows are his own.
   He sustains the hidden life
   Safe with him from earthly strife.

5. O my Savior, help afford
   By your spirit and your Word!
   When my wayward heart would stray,
   Keep me in the narrow way;
   Grace in time of need supply
   While I live and when I die.
   (*LW* 285)

Text: William McComb

Christ, the Life
of All the Living

1. Christ, the Life of all the living,
   Christ, the Death of death, our foe,
   Who, Thyself for me once giving
   To the darkest depths of woe:
   Through thy sufferings, death, and merit
   I eternal life inherit:
   Thousand, thousand thanks shall be,
   Dearest Jesus, unto Thee.

2. Thou, ah! Thou, hast taken on Thee
   Bonds and stripes, a cruel rod;
   Pain and scorn were heaped upon Thee,
   O Thou sinless Son of God!
   Thus didst Thou my soul deliver
   From the bonds of sin forever.
   Thousand, thousand thanks shall be,
   Dearest Jesus, unto Thee.

3. Thou hast borne the smiting only
   That my wounds might all be whole;
   Thou hast suffered, sad and lonely,
   Rest to give my weary soul;
   Yea, the curse of God enduring,
   Blessing unto me securing.
   Thousand, thousand thanks shall be,
   Dearest Jesus, unto Thee.

4. Heartless scoffers did surround Thee,
   Treating Thee with shameful scorn,
   And with piercing thorns they crowned Thee.
   All disgrace Thou, Lord, hast borne
   That as Thine Thou mightest own me
   And with heavenly glory crown me.
   Thousand, thousand thanks shall be,
   Dearest Jesus, unto Thee.

5. Thou hast suffered men to bruise Thee
   That from pain I might be free;
   Falsely did Thy foes accuse Thee,—
   Thence I gain security;
   Comfortless Thy soul did languish
   Me to comfort in my anguish.
   Thousand, thousand thanks shall be,
   Dearest Jesus, unto Thee.

6. Thou hast suffered great affliction
   And hast borne it patiently,
   Even death by crucifixion,
   Fully to atone for me;
   Thou didst choose to be tormented
   That my doom should be prevented.
   Thousand, thousand thanks shall be,
   Dearest Jesus, unto Thee.

7. Then, for all that wrought my pardon,
   For Thy sorrows deep and sore,
   For Thine anguish in the Garden,
   I will thank Thee evermore,
   Thank Thee for Thy groaning, sighing,
   For Thy bleeding and Thy dying,
   For that last triumphant cry,
   And shall praise Thee, Lord, on high. (*TLH* 151)

Text: Ernst C. Homburg

Go, My Children, with My Blessing

1. Go, My children, with My blessing, Never alone.
   Waking, sleeping, I am with you; You are My own.
   In My love's baptismal river I have made you Mine forever.
   Go, My children, with My blessing, You are My own.

2. Go, My children, sins forgiven, At peace and pure.
   Here you learned how much I love you, What I can cure.
   Here you heard My dear Son's story;
          Here you touched Him, saw His glory.
   Go, My children, sins forgiven, At peace and pure.

3. Go, My children, fed and nourished, Closer to Me;
   Grow in love and love by serving, Joyful and free.
   Here My Spirit's power filled you;
      Here His tender comfort stilled you.
   Go, My children, fed and nourished, Joyful and free.

4. I the Lord will bless and keep you And give you peace;
   I the Lord will smile upon you And give you peace;
   I the Lord will be your Father, Savior, Comforter, and Brother.
   Go, My Children; I will keep you And give you peace. (*HS 887*)

Text: Jaroslav Vajda

> If through love He Himself is with us on earth,
> then through this same love we are with Him in
> heaven. . . He is therefore below, and we are
> above: He is below through the compassion of
> love, we are above through the hope of love."
> —Augustine[16]

God's Own Child, I Gladly Say It

1. God's own child, I gladly say it:
   I am baptized into Christ!
   He, because I could not pay it,
   Gave my full redemption price.
   Do I need earth's treasures many?
   I have one worth more than any
   That brought me salvation free
   Lasting to eternity!

2. Sin, disturb my soul no longer:
   I am baptized into Christ!
   I have comfort even stronger:
   Jesus' cleansing sacrifice.
   Should a guilty conscience seize me
   Since my Baptism did release me
   In a dear forgiving flood,
   Sprinkling me with Jesus' blood?

3. Satan hear this proclamation:
   I am baptized into Christ!
   Drop your ugly accusation,
   I am not so soon enticed.
   Now that to the font I've traveled,
   All your might has come unraveled,
   And, against your tyranny,
   God, my Lord, unites with me!

4. Death, you cannot end my gladness:
   I am baptized into Christ!
   When I die, I leave all sadness
   To inherit paradise!
   Though I lie in dust and ashes
   Faith's assurance brightly flashes!
   Baptism has the strength divine
   To make life immortal mine.

5. There is nothing worth comparing
   To this lifelong comfort sure!
   Open-eyed my grave is staring;
   Even there I'll sleep secure.
   Though my flesh awaits its raising,
   Still my soul continues praising
   I am baptized into Christ;
   I'm a child of paradise!
   (*HS* 844)

Text: Erdmann Neumeister

37

Here Is the Tenfold Sure Command

1. Here is the tenfold sure command
   God gave to men of ev'ry land
   Through faithful Moses standing high
   On holy Mount Sinai
   Have mercy, Lord!

2. "I, I alone am God, your Lord;
   All idols are to be abhorred.
   Trust me, step boldly to my throne,
   Sincerely love me alone."
   Have mercy, Lord!

3. "Do not My holy name disgrace,
   Do not My Word of truth debase.
   Praise only that as good and true
   Which I Myself say and do."
   Have mercy, Lord!

4. "And celebrate the worship day
   That peace may fill your home, and pray,
   And put aside the work you do,
   So that God may work in you."
   Have mercy, Lord!

5. "You are to honor and obey
   Your father, mother, ev'ry day,
   Serve them each way that comes to hand;
   You'll then live long in the land."
   Have mercy, Lord!

6. "Curb anger, do not harm or kill,
   Hate not, repay not ill with ill.
   Be patient and of gentle mind,
   Convince your foe you are kind."
   Have mercy, Lord!

7. "Be faithful, keep your marriage vow;
   The straying thought do not allow.
   Keep all your conduct free from sin
   By self-controlled discipline."
   Have mercy, Lord!

8. "You shall not steal or take away
   What others worked for night and day,
   But open wide a gen'rous hand
   And help the poor in the land."
   Have mercy, Lord!

9. "A lying witness never be,
   Nor foul your tongue with calumny.
   The cause of innocence embrace,
   The fallen shield from disgrace."
   Have mercy, Lord!

10. "The portion in your neighbor's lot,
    His goods, home, wife, desire not.
    Pray God He would your neighbor bless
    As you yourself wish success."
    Have mercy, Lord!

11. You have this law to see therein
    That you have not been free from sin
    But also that you clearly see
    How pure toward God life should be.
    Have mercy, Lord!

12. Our works cannot salvation gain;
    They merit only endless pain.
    Forgive us, Lord! To Christ we flee,
    Who pleads for us endlessly.
    Have mercy, Lord! (*LW* 331)

Text: Martin Luther

Jesus Christ
Is Risen Today

1. Jesus Christ is risen today, Alleluia!
   Our triumphant holy day, Alleluia!
   Who did once upon the cross, Alleluia!
   Suffer to redeem our loss. Alleluia!

2. Hymns of praise then let us sing, Alleluia!
   Unto Christ, our heavenly king, Alleluia!
   Who endured the cross and grave, Alleluia!
   Sinners to redeem and save. Alleluia!

3. But the pains which he endured, Alleluia!
   Our salvation have procured; Alleluia!
   Now above the sky he's king, Alleluia!
   Where the angels ever sing. Alleluia!

4. Sing we to our God above, Alleluia!
   Praise eternal as his love; Alleluia!
   Praise him, all you heavenly host, Alleluia!
   Father, Son, and Holy Ghost. Alleluia! (*LW* 127)

Latin carol, 14th cent.

Nations pass away, but the church
continues. Where there is a people
which no longer has a future, there
the church still has a future, because
the future of the church is the future
of Jesus Christ.

—Hermann Sasse[18]

Jesus, Your Blood and Righteousness

Faith, Justification

1. Jesus, your blood and righteousness
   My beauty are, my glorious dress;
   Mid flaming worlds, in these arrayed,
   With joy shall I lift up my head.

2. Bold shall I stand in that great day,
   Cleansed and redeemed, no debt to pay
   For by your cross absolved I am
   From sin and guilt, from fear and shame.

3. Lord, I believe your precious blood,
   Which at the mercy seat of God
   Pleads for the captives' liberty,
   Was also shed in love for me.

4. Lord, I believe were sinners more
   Than sands upon the ocean shore,
   You have for all a ransom paid,
   For all a full atonement made.

5. When from the dust of death I rise
   To claim my mansion in the skies,
   This then shall be my only plea:
   Christ Jesus lived and died for me.

6. Then shall I praise you and adore,
   Your blessed name forevermore,
   Who once, for me and all you made,
   An everlasting ransom paid. (*LW* 362)

Text: Ludwig von Zinzendorf

Joy to the World

1. Joy to the world, the Lord is come!
   Let earth receive her King;
   Let every heart prepare Him room
   And heaven and nature sing.

2. Joy to the earth, the Savior reigns!
   Let men their songs employ,
   While fields and floods, rocks, hills, and plains
   Repeat the sounding joy.

3. No more let sins and sorrows grow
   Nor thorns infest the ground;
   He comes to make His blessings flow
   Far as the curse is found.

4. He rules the world with truth and grace
   And makes the nations prove
   The glories of His righteousness
   And wonders of His love. (*TLH* 87)

Text: Isaac Watts

Behold the church! It is the very opposite of loneliness—
blessed fellowship! There are millions of saints and believers who are blessed in it, and in the midst of their songs
of praise is the Lord. No longer lonely, but filled, satisfied,
yes, blessed he who is one of these millions who com-
pletely and fully have Christ and with him
heaven and earth!

—Wilhelm Loehe[13]

O Holy, Blessed Trinity

1. O holy, blessed Trinity,
   Divine, eternal Unity,
   O Father, Son, and Holy Ghost,
   This day your name be uppermost.

2. My soul and body keep from harm,
   And over all extend your arm;
   Let Satan cause me no distress
   Nor bring me shame and wretchedness.

3. The Father's love shield me this day;
   The Son's pure wisdom cheer my way;
   The Holy Spirit's joy and light
   Drive from my heart the shades of night.

4. My Maker, hold me in your hand;
   O Christ, forgiven let me stand;
   Blest Comforter, do not depart,
   With faith and love enrich my heart.

5. Lord, bless and keep me as your own;
   Lord, look in kindness from your throne;
   Lord, shine unfailing peace on me
   By grace surrounded; set me free. (*LW* 479)

Text: Martin Behm

Salvation
unto Us Has Come

1. Salvation unto us has come
   By God's free grace and favor;
   Good works cannot avert our doom,
   They help and save us never.
   Faith looks to Jesus Christ alone,
   Who did for all the world atone;
   He is our one redeemer.

2. What God did in his Law demand
   And none to him could render
   Caused wrath and woe on ev'ry hand
   For man, the vile offender.
   Our flesh has not those pure desires
   The spirit of the Law requires,
   And lost is our condition.

3. It was a false, misleading dream
   That God his Law had given
   That sinners could themselves redeem
   And by their works gain heaven.
   The Law is but a mirror bright
   To bring the inbred sin to light
   That lurks within our nature.

4. Since Christ has full atonement made
   And brought to us salvation,
   Each Christian therefore may be glad
   And build on this foundation.
   Your grace alone, dear Lord, I plead,
   Your death is now my life indeed,
   For you have paid my ransom

5. Faith clings to Jesus' cross alone
   And rests in him unceasing;
   And by its fruits true faith is known,
   With love and hope increasing.
   For faith alone can justify;
   Works serve our neighbor and supply
   The proof that faith is living.

6. All blessing, honor, thanks, and praise
   To Father, Son, and Spirit,
   The God who saved us by his grace;
   All glory to his merit.
   O triune God in heav'n above,
   You have revealed your saving love;
   Your blessed name we hallow. (*LW* 355)

Text: Paul Speratus

> You stir man to take pleasure in
> praising You, because You have
> made us for Yourself, and our heart
> is restless until it rests in You.
> — Augustine[14]

Silent Night

1. Silent night! Holy night!
   All is calm, all is bright,
   Round yon Virgin Mother and Child.
   Holy Infant, so tender and mild,
   Sleep in heavenly peace,
   Sleep in heavenly peace.

2. Silent night! Holy night!
   Shepherds quake at the sight;
   Glories stream from heaven afar,
   Heavenly hosts sing, Alleluia.
   Christ, the Savior, is born!
   Christ, the Savior, is born!

3. Silent night! Holy night!
   Son of God, love's pure light
   Radiant beams from Thy holy face,
   With the dawn of redeeming grace,
   Jesus, Lord, at Thy birth.
   Jesus, Lord, at Thy birth. (*TLH 646*)

Text: Joseph Mohr

Faith that God is for me in every
way is God's antidote to the worry
that undermines inner joy.
— Henry Hamann[15]

Songs of Thankfulness and Praise

1. Songs of thankfulness and
     praise,
   Jesus, Lord, to thee we raise,
   Manifested by the star
   To the sages from afar,
   Branch of royal David's
     stem,
   In thy birth at Bethlehem:
   Anthems be to thee
     addressed,
   God in flesh made manifest.

2. Manifest at Jordan's stream,
   Prophet, Priest, and King
     supreme,
   And at Cana, wedding
     guest,
   In thy Godhead manifest;
   Manifest in pow'r divine,
   Changing water into wine.
   Anthems be to thee
     addressed,
   God in flesh made manifest.

3. Manifest in making whole
   Palsied limbs and fainting
     soul;
   Manifest in valiant fight,
   Quelling all the devil's
     might;
   Manifest in gracious will,
   Ever bringing good from ill.
   Anthems be to thee
     addressed,
   God in flesh made manifest.

4. Grant us grace to see thee,
     Lord,
   Present in thy holy Word;
   Grace to imitate thee now
   And be pure as pure art thou
   That we might become like
     thee
   At thy great epiphany
   And may praise thee, ever
     blest,
   God in flesh made manifest.
   (*LW* 88)

   Text: Christopher Wordsworth

Thy Strong Word

1. Thy strong word did cleave the darkness;
   At thy speaking it was done.
   For created light we thank thee,
   While thine ordered seasons run.
   Alleluia, alleluia!
   Praise to thee who light dost send!
   Alleluia, alleluia!
   Alleluia without end!

2. Lo, on those who dwelt in darkness,
   Dark as night and deep as death,
   Broke the light of thy salvation,
   Breathed thine own life-breathing breath.
   Alleluia, alleluia!
   Praise to thee who light dost send!
   Alleluia, alleluia!
   Alleluia without end!

3. Thy strong Word bespeaks us righteous;
   Bright with thine own holiness,
   Glorious now, we press toward glory,
   And our lives our hopes confess.
   Alleluia, alleluia!
   Praise to thee who light dost send!
   Alleluia, alleluia!
   Alleluia without end!

4. From the cross thy wisdom shining
   Breaketh forth in conqu'ring might;
   From the cross forever beameth
   All thy bright redeeming light.
   Alleluia, alleluia!
   Praise to thee who light dost send!
   Alleluia, alleluia!
   Alleluia without end!

5. Give us lips to sing thy glory,
   Tongues thy mercy to proclaim
   Throats that shout the hope that fills us,
   Mouths to speak thy holy name.
   Alleluia, alleluia!
   May the light which thou dost send
   Fill our songs with alleluias,
   Alleluia without end!

6. God the Father, light-creator,
   To thee laud and honor be.
   To thee, Light of Light begotten,
   Praise be sung eternally.
   Holy Spirit, light-revealer,
   Glory, glory be to thee.
   Mortals, angels, now and ever
   Praise the holy Trinity! (*LW* 328)

Text: Martin H. Franzmann

With the Lord
Begin Your Task

1. With the Lord begin your task;
   Jesus will direct it.
   For his aid and counsel ask;
   Jesus will perfect it.
   Every morn with Jesus rise,
   And when day is ended,
   In his name then close your eyes;
   Be to him commended.

2. Let each day begin with prayer,
   Praise, and adoration.
   On the Lord cast every care;
   He is your salvation.
   Morning, evening, and at night
   Jesus will be near you,
   Save you from the tempter's might,
   With his presence cheer you.

3. With the Savior at your side,
   Foes need not alarm you;
   In his promises confide,
   And no ill can harm you.
   All your trust and hope repose
   In the mighty master,
   Who in wisdom truly knows
   How to stem disaster.

4. If your task be thus begun
   With the Savior's blessing,
   Safely then your course will run,
   Toward the promise pressing.
   Good will follow ev'rywhere
   While you here must wander.
   You at last the joy will share
   In the mansions yonder. (*LW* 483)

Text: Morgen-und Abend-segen

On the third day the friends of Christ coming at
day-break to the place found the grave empty
and the stone rolled away. In varying ways they
realized the new wonder; but even they hardly
realized that the world had died in the night.
What they were looking at was the first day of a
new creation, with a new heaven and a new
earth; and in a semblance of the gardener God
walked again in the garden, in the cool not of the
evening but the dawn.

—G. K. Chesterton[17]

Dr. Martin Luther was always up to date with his deep spiritual insights. In discussing the First Commandment in his Large Catechism, he wrote:

. . .I have often said, the trust and faith of the heart alone make both God and an idol. If your faith and trust are right, then your God is the true God. On the other hand, if your trust is false and wrong, then you have not the true God. For these two belong together, faith and God. That to which your heart clings and entrusts itself is, I say, really your God.

Let everyone, then, take care to magnify and exalt this commandment above all things and not make light of it. Search and examine your own heart thoroughly and you will find whether or not it clings to God alone. Do you have the kind of heart that expects from him nothing but good, especially in distress and want, and renounces and forsakes all that is not God? Then you have the one true God. On the contrary, does your heart cling to something else, from which it hopes to receive more good and help than from God, and does it flee not to him but from him when things go wrong? Then you have an idol, another god.[20]

The great reformer knew the university of his day thoroughly, both as a student and as a professor. Luther, we can say, anticipated our times too. Today campus idols are plentiful and evoke all kinds of devotion and service. Think of a few of the better known from the campus pantheon: Scientism, Humanism, Relativism, Intellectualism, Successism, Statusism. If we believe in any of these, or others, as representing the most important—apart from the Creator—we have displaced Him with new gods, new "creators." The result, to paraphrase Luther's thought: "whatever comes between you and God is your god."

Our God has demonstrated that He is not only Creator but also Redeemer in Jesus Christ. Jesus Christ is God seeking and finding people through His Word, having already reconciled them to God on the cross. Jesus bore your sin too, including recurrent loyalties to the false idols and "isms" that lie in wait for you on campus and the workplace. God in His love continues to restore those who look to Christ as Savior.

By living as a college confessor of Jesus, you can keep your worship and your life focused on the true Creator and Lord. You can live in fellowship with God through Word and Sacrament. You can direct your worship and service to Him with prayer, and so live with true perspective. Such a practical devotional life informs campus experience and lines up values and goals in a realistic manner. Let the Creator guide your heart, mind, and life.[21]

Creator Spirit, by whose aid
The world's foundations first
    were laid,
Come, visit every humble mind;
Come, pour your joys on
    humankind;
From sin and sorrow set us free;
May we, each one, your temple
    be.

Immortal honor, endless fame
Attend the gracious Father's
    name;
The Savior Son be glorified,
Who for lost man's redemption
    died;
And equal adoration rise
For you, O Spirit, to the skies.
    (*LW* 167)

Text: attr. Rhabanus Maurus,
tr. John Dryden

The Benedictus (Zechariah's Song)

Blessed be the Lord God of Israel; for He has visited and redeemed His people and has raised up a horn of salvation for us in the house of His servant David, as He spoke by the mouth of His holy prophets, who have been since the world began. That we should be saved from our enemies and from the hand of all who hate us; to perform the mercy promised to our fathers and remember His holy covenant, the oath that He swore to our father Abraham, to grant us that we, being delivered from the hand of our enemies, might serve Him without fear, in holiness and righteousness before Him all the days of our life.

[During Advent:] And you, child, will be called the prophet of the Most High; for you will go before the Lord to prepare His ways, to give knowledge of salvation to His people in the forgiveness of their sins, through the tender mercy of our God; when the day shall dawn upon us from on high to give light to them who sit in darkness and in the shadow of death, to guide our feet in the way of peace.

Nunc dimittis (Simeon's Song)

Lord, now let your servant depart in peace according to your word, for my eyes have seen your salvation, which you have prepared before the face of all people, a Light to lighten the Gentiles, and the glory of Your people Israel.

Glory be to the Father and to the Son and to the Holy Spirit; as it was in the beginning, is now, and will be forever. Amen.

Te Deum laudamus

We praise You, O God; we acknowledge You to be the Lord; all the earth now worships You, the Father everlasting. To You all angels cry aloud, the heavens and all the powers therein.

To You cherubim and seraphim continually do cry: Holy, holy, holy, Lord God of Sabaoth; heaven and earth are full of the majesty of Your glory. The glorious company of the apostles praise You; the goodly fellowship of the prophets praise You. The noble army of martyrs praise You. The holy Church throughout all the world does acknowledge You:

The Father of an infinite majesty; Your adorable true and only Son, also the Holy Ghost, the comforter. You are the King of glory, O Christ; You are the everlasting Son of the Father.

When You took upon Yourself to deliver man, You humbled Yourself to be born of a virgin. When You had overcome the sharpness of death, You opened the kingdom of heaven to all believers. You sit at the right hand of God in the glory of the Father. We believe that You will come to be our judge.

We therefore pray You to help Your servants, whom You have redeemed with your precious blood. Make them to be numbered with Your saints in glory everlasting.

O Lord, save Your people and bless Your heritage. Govern them up forever. Day by day we magnify You. And we worship Your name ever, world without end. Vouchsafe, O Lord, to keep us this day without sin. O Lord, have mercy upon us, have mercy upon us. O Lord, let Your mercy be upon us, as our trust is in You. O Lord, in You have I trusted; let me never be confounded.

> It is because the same old thing keeps on being preached, the apostles' doctrine, that the church keeps on living.
> —Hermann Sasse[23]

The Magnificat (Mary's Song)

My soul magnifies the Lord, and my spirit rejoices in God, my Savior; for He has regarded the lowliness of His handmaiden. For, behold, from this day all generations will call me blessed. For the Mighty One has done great things to me, and Holy is His name; and His mercy is on those who fear Him from generation to generation. He has shown strength with His arm; He has scattered the proud in the imagination of their hearts. He has cast down the mighty from their thrones, and has exalted the lowly. He has filled the hungry with good things, and the rich He has sent away empty. He has helped His servant Israel in remembrance of His mercy, as He spoke to our fathers, to Abraham, and to his seed forever.

Venite

Oh, come, let us sing to the Lord, let us make a joyful noise to the Rock of our salvation.

Let us come into His presence with thanksgiving, let us make a joyful noise to Him with songs of praise. For the Lord is a great God and a great King above all gods. The deep places of the earth are in His hands; the strength of the hills is His also. The sea is His, and He made it; and His hands formed the dry land. Oh, come, let us worship and bow down, let us kneel before the Lord our maker. For He is our God, and we are the people of His pasture and the sheep of His hand.

Glory be to the Father and to the Son and to the Holy Spirit; as it was in the beginning, is now, and will be forever. Amen.

> Faith that exercises itself in holiness is just the faith that turns a person to repentance and teaches the one who is doing good works to seek after the promises of forgiveness."
> —Albert Koberle [24]

That's-All-There-Is-
There-Ain't-No-More-ism

One of the truly attractive idols of our day is "scientific humanism." It is also called by some "naturalistic humanism." This credo, popular among some scholars, claims that the only true knowledge is that which is found by means of the scientific method. Only truths verified by the ground rules of this "religion" are real truths. (And is such a dogma itself so verified?) Only that which can be perceived and understood empirically really exists—nothing else is known for sure.

A Christian values the blessings of science as man has found and benefited by them. But he recognizes from whom they have come and who has given us the resources to develop them. The Christian is broad-minded enough to allow for knowledge that cannot be "proved" by rational and purely empirical means. Indeed, the Christian believes in such knowledge. It is knowledge that is not against reason. It is knowledge that expresses dimensions of life and purpose that are above man's reasoning capabilities. The church humbly expresses its creed to the world. Meanwhile the adherents of a narrow humanistic view, which replaces God with man, claim that what science has done proves the theme "that's-all-there-is-there-ain't-no-more. "

Greater insight than this belongs to the well-informed Christian student. He knows whom He has believed and is sure that He is able to guard until the Last Day what has been entrusted to Him. His faith is centered in the person and work of Jesus Christ, of whom St. John said, "All things were made through Him, and without Him was not any thing made that was made. In Him was life, and the life was the light of men" (John 1:3–4). God in His love takes His creation so seriously that He entered human life in Jesus Christ to restore mankind to His highest purposes: fellowship with God, love, and fulfillment. Eternal life is given to man.

Pursuing knowledge with a Christian mind is to be set free from the worship of the idol of scientism or a narrow rationalism. It is to be set free to worship God and to develop as His creature. It is to be set free from the philosophy that shackles the minds of those whose little knowledge of science leads them to worship it as omnipotent. It is to hear the Savior calling to His own in the academic world: "If you abide in My word, you are truly My disciples, and you will know the truth, and the truth will set you free. . . .if the Son sets you free, you will be free indeed." (John 8:31–32,36)[25]

All depends on our possessing
God's free grace and constant blessing,
Though all earthly wealth depart.
They who trust with faith unshaken
By their God are not forsaken
And will keep a dauntless heart.

He who to this day has fed me
And to many joys has led me
Is and ever shall be mine.
He who did so gently school me,
He who daily guides and rules me
Will remain my help divine.

Well he knows what best to grant me
All the longing hopes that haunt me,
Joy and sorrow have their day.
I shall doubt his wisdom never;
As God wills so be it ever;
I commit to him my way. (*LW* 415:1,2,5)

Text: Gesang-Buch, tr. Catherine Winkworth

SELECTION OF
Psalms

Jesus Christ feeds us in the desert places of our lives.
He feeds us with his Word and the precious Sacrament.
You might feel like you're deserted, but you're not.
The Savior still comes to feed us in those private
wildernesses of our lives. Alone with sin is not good.
But alone with God is very good. In those desert
places within, Jesus Christ still feeds His people with
His forgiveness, with His life, and with His salvation.
—Harold L. Senkbeil [26]

THEMES IN THE SELECTED PSALMS

Assurance	Psalm 119:9–16; 121
Close of Day	Psalm 16:1–5, 10–14
Confession	Psalm 51
Consolation and Comfort	Psalm 38:9, 21–22; 90
Danger	Psalm 143
Evening	Psalm 46
Forgiveness	Psalm 32, 119:33–46
Marriage	Psalm 127
Mercy	Psalm 6, 130:1–6, 142
Morning	Psalm 100
Penitential Psalms	Psalm 6, 32, 38, 51, 102, 130, 143
Praise	Psalm 30, 138
Righteousness	Psalm 1
Trouble	Psalm 6, 38, 102
Trust	Psalm 23, 130

OTHER PSALMS FOR DAILY PRAYER

Morning Prayer

Sundays and Festivals:	Psalm 1, 2, 8, 19, 27, 45, 62, 67, 72, 84, 98
Other Days:	Psalm 5, 18, 22, 24, 25, 28, 36, 50, 65, 73, 90, 92, 96, 100, 107, 119, 147, 148

Evening Prayer

Sundays and Festivals:	Psalm 23, 110, 111, 114
Other Days:	Psalm 6, 46, 51, 105, 116, 117, 118, 126, 130, 135, 136, 138, 139, 141, 143, 146

Close of the Day

Sundays and Festivals:	Psalm 91, 133, 134
Other Days:	Psalm 4, 12, 16, 18, 24, 34, 77, 103, 121

Laudate Psalms

Sunday	Psalm 150
Monday	Psalm 145
Tuesday	Psalm 146
Wednesday	Psalm 147:1–11
Thursday	Psalm 147:12–20
Friday	Psalm 148
Saturday	Psalm 149

Penitential Psalms: Psalm 6, 32, 38, 51, 102, 130, 143

THEMES IN CHRISTIAN LIFE

Affliction:	Psalm 34, 130
Comfort:	Psalm 116, 118
Confession:	Psalm 30, 102
Confidence and Trust:	Psalm 16, 25, 27, 37, 62, 91, 121, 139
Encouragement:	Psalm 73
Eternal Life:	Psalm 16, 17, 49, 116
Forgiveness:	Psalm 103
Marriage:	Psalm 45, 127
Mercy:	Psalm 6, 25, 32, 36, 38, 73, 77, 102, 143
Praise:	Psalm 9, 18, 32, 40, 66, 92, 98, 100, 116, 145
Prayer:	Psalm 17, 86, 90, 102, 142
Thanksgiving:	Psalm 30, 31, 100, 116, 124, 126, 136
Trust:	Psalm 27, 62, 63, 71, 131
Salvation:	Psalm 40, 67, 128
Strength in the Face of Tribulation:	Psalm 3, 5, 10, 43, 54, 57, 77

TABLE OF PSALMS FOR DAILY PRAYER

	Saturday	Sunday	Monday	Tuesday
Advent Morning Prayer		24, 150	122, 145	33, 146
Evening Prayer	80, 72	25, 110	40, 67	85, 94

Christmas		Morning Prayer	Evening Prayer
	December 24		102, 114
	December 25	2, Laudate	98, 96
	December 26	116, Laudate	119:1–24, 27
	December 27	34, Laudate	19, 121
	December 28	2, Laudate	110, 111
	December 29	96, Laudate	132, 97
	December 30	93, Laudate	89:1–18, 89:19–52

	Saturday	Sunday	Monday	Tuesday
Lent Morning Prayer		84, 150	119:73–80; 145	34, 146
Evening Prayer	31, 143	42, 32	121, 6	25, 91
Easter Morning Prayer		93, 150	97, 145	98, 146
Evening Prayer	23, 114	136, 117	124, 115	66, 116
General— Week 1 Morning Prayer		5–8	12–16	19–21
Evening Prayer	1–4	9–11	17, 18	22–24
General— Week 2 Morning Prayer		50–53	57–60	65–67
Evening Prayer	46–49	54–56	61–64	68
General— Week 3 Morning Prayer		89	93, 94, 96	102, 103
Evening Prayer	86–88	90–92	97–101	104
General— Week 4 Morning Prayer		119:33–64	119:97–136	120–124
Evening Prayer	119:1-32	119:65–96	119:137–176	125–129

Wednesday	Thursday	Friday	Saturday
50, 147:1–12	18:1–20; 147:13–21	102, 148	90, 149
53, 17	136, 62	130, 16	

		Morning Prayer	Evening Prayer
	December 31	98, Laudate	45, 96
	January 1	98, Laudate	99, 8
	January 2	48, Laudate	9, 29
	January 3	111, Laudate	107, 15
	January 4	20, Laudate	93, 97
	January 5	99, Laudate	96, 110
	January 6	72, Laudate	100, 67

Wednesday	Thursday	Friday	Saturday
5, 147:1–12	27, 147:13–21	22, 148	43, 149
27, 51	126, 102	105, 130	
99, 137:1–12	47, 147:13–21	96, 148	92, 149
9, 118	68, 113	49, 138	
25–27	31–33	37, 38	43–45
28–30	34–36	39–42	
69	73, 74	78	82–85
70–72	75–77	79–81	
105	107, 108	111–114	118
106	109, 110	115–117	
130–133	136–138	143–145	148–150
134–125	139–142	146, 147	

Righteousness

Blessed is the man
    who walks not in the counsel of the wicked,
nor stands in the way of sinners,
    nor sits in the seat of scoffers;
2but His delight is in the law of the LORD,
    and on his law he meditates day and night.
3He is like a tree
    planted by streams of water
that yields its fruit in its season,
    and its leaf does not wither.
In all that he does, he prospers.
4The wicked are not so,
    but are like chaff that the wind drives away.
5Therefore the wicked will not stand in the judgment,
    nor sinners in the congregation of the righteous;
6for the LORD knows the way of the righteous,
    but the way of the wicked will perish.

In Time of Trouble

O LORD, rebuke me not in Your anger,
    nor discipline me in Your wrath.
2Be gracious to me, O LORD, for I am languishing;
    heal me, O LORD, for my bones are troubled.
3My soul also is greatly troubled.
    But You, O LORD—how long?
4Turn, O LORD, deliver my life;
    save me for the sake of Your steadfast love.

⁵For in death there is no remembrance of You;
    in Sheol who will give You praise?
⁶I am weary with my moaning;
    every night I flood my bed with tears;
    I drench my couch with my weeping.
⁷My eye wastes away because of grief;
    it grows weak because of all my foes.
⁸Depart from me, all you workers of evil,
    for the LORD has heard the sound of my weeping.
⁹The LORD has heard my plea;
    the LORD accepts my prayer.
¹⁰All my enemies shall be ashamed and greatly
       troubled;
    they shall turn back and be put to shame in
      a moment.

Close of Day   *Psalm 16:1–5, 10–11*

Preserve me, O God, for in You I take refuge.
²I say to the LORD, "You are my Lord;
    I have no good apart from You."
³As for the saints in the land, they are the excellent
      ones,
    in whom is all my delight.
⁴The sorrows of those who run after another god
      shall multiply;
    their drink offerings of blood I will not pour out
    or take their names on my lips.
⁵The LORD is my chosen portion and my cup;
    You hold my lot.

¹⁰For You will not abandon my soul to Sheol,
   or let Your holy one see corruption.
¹¹You make known to me the path of life;
   in Your presence there is fullness of joy;
   at Your right hand are pleasures forevermore.

Trust   *Psalm 23*

The LORD is my shepherd; I shall not want.
   ²He makes me lie down in green pastures.
He leads me beside still waters.
   ³He restores my soul.
He leads me in paths of righteousness
   for His name's sake.
⁴Even though I walk through the valley of the
            shadow of death,
   I will fear no evil,
for You are with me;
   Your rod and Your staff,
   they comfort me.
⁵You prepare a table before me
   in the presence of my enemies;
You anoint my head with oil;
   my cup overflows.
⁶Surely goodness and mercy shall follow me
   all the days of my life,
and I shall dwell in the house of the LORD
   forever.

I will extol You, O Lord, for You have drawn me up
   and have not let my foes rejoice over me.
²O Lord my God, I cried to You for help,
   and You have healed me.
³O Lord, You have brought up my soul from Sheol;
   You restored me to life from among those
      who go down to the pit.
   ⁴Sing praises to the Lord, O you His saints,
and give thanks to His holy name.
   ⁵For His anger is but for a moment,
and His favor is for a lifetime.
   Weeping may tarry for the night,
but joy comes with the morning.
   ⁶As for me, I said in my prosperity,
"I shall never be moved."
   ⁷By Your favor, O Lord,
You made my mountain stand strong;
   You hid Your face;
I was dismayed.
⁸To You, O Lord, I cry,
   and to the Lord I plead for mercy:
⁹"What profit is there in my death,
   if I go down to the pit?
Will the dust praise You?
   Will it tell of Your faithfulness?
¹⁰Hear, O Lord, and be merciful to me!
   O Lord, be my helper!"
¹¹You have turned for me my mourning
      into dancing;

You have loosed my sackcloth
and clothed me with gladness,
[12]that my glory may sing Your praise
and not be silent.
O LORD my God, I will give thanks to You forever!

Joy of Forgiveness

Psalm 32

Blessed is the one whose transgression is forgiven,
whose sin is covered.
[2]Blessed is the man against whom the LORD
counts no iniquity,
and in whose spirit there is no deceit.
[3]For when I kept silent, my bones wasted away
through my groaning all day long.
[4]For day and night Your hand was heavy upon me;
my strength was dried up as by the heat
of summer. *Selah*
[5]I acknowledged my sin to You,
and I did not cover my iniquity;
I said, "I will confess my transgressions
to the LORD,"
and You forgave the iniquity of my sin. *Selah*
[6]Therefore let everyone who is godly
offer prayer to You at a time when You may be
found;
surely in the rush of great waters,
they shall not reach Him.
[7]You are a hiding place for me;
You preserve me from trouble;

You surround me with shouts of deliverance.
Selah

⁸I will instruct you and teach you in the way
    you should go;
  I will counsel you with My eye upon you.
⁹Be not like a horse or a mule,
    without understanding,
  which must be curbed with bit and bridle,
  or it will not stay near you.
¹⁰Many are the sorrows of the wicked,
  but steadfast love surrounds the one who trusts
        in the LORD.
¹¹Be glad in the LORD, and rejoice, O righteous,
  and shout for joy, all you upright in heart!

Consolation and Comfort   *Psalm 38*

O LORD, rebuke me not in Your anger,
  nor discipline me in Your wrath!
²For Your arrows have sunk into me,
  and Your hand has come down on me.
³There is no soundness in my flesh
  because of Your indignation;
there is no health in my bones
  because of my sin.
⁴For my iniquities have gone over my head;
  like a heavy burden, they are too heavy for me.
⁵My wounds stink and fester
  because of my foolishness,
⁶I am utterly bowed down and prostrate;

all the day I go about mourning.
⁷For my sides are filled with burning,
    and there is no soundness in my flesh.
⁸I am feeble and crushed;
    I groan because of the tumult of my heart.
⁹O Lord, all my longing is before You;
    my sighing is not hidden from You.
¹⁰My heart throbs; my strength fails me,
    and the light of my eyes—it also has gone
                        from me.
¹¹My friends and companions stand aloof
                    from my plague,
    and my nearest kin stand far off.
¹²Those who seek my life lay their snares;
    those who seek my hurt speak of ruin
    and meditate treachery all day long.
¹³But I am like a deaf man; I do not hear,
    like a mute man who does not open his mouth.
¹⁴I have become like a man who does not hear,
    and in whose mouth are no rebukes.
¹⁵But for You, O LORD, do I wait;
    it is You, O Lord my God, who will answer.
¹⁶For I said, "Only let them not rejoice over me,
    who boast against me when my foot slips!"
¹⁷For I am ready to fall,
    and my pain is ever before me.
¹⁸I confess my iniquity;
    I am sorry for my sin.
¹⁹But my foes are vigorous, they are mighty,
    and many are those who hate me wrongfully.
²⁰Those who render me evil for good

accuse me because I follow after good.
²¹Do not forsake me, O LORD!
   O my God, be not far from me!
²²Make haste to help me,
   O Lord, my salvation!

Evening   *Psalm 46*

God is our refuge and strength,
   a very present help in trouble.
²Therefore we will not fear though the earth gives
      way,
   though the mountains be moved into the heart
         of the sea,
³though its waters roar and foam,
   though the mountains tremble at its swelling.
                    Selah
⁴There is a river whose streams make glad the city
      of God,
   the holy habitation of the Most High.
⁵God is in the midst of her; she shall not be moved;
   God will help her when morning dawns.
⁶The nations rage, the kingdoms totter;
   He utters His voice, the earth melts.
⁷The LORD of hosts is with us;
   the God of Jacob is our fortress. *Selah*
⁸Come, behold the works of the LORD,
   how He has brought desolations on the earth.
⁹He makes wars cease to the end of the earth;
   He breaks the bow and shatters the spear;

He burns the chariots with fire.
10"Be still, and know that I am God.
   I will be exalted among the nations,
   I will be exalted in the earth!"
11The LORD of hosts is with us;
   the God of Jacob is our fortress.

Prayer for Forgiveness - Confession   *Psalm 51*

Have mercy on me, O God,
   according to Your steadfast love;
according to Your abundant mercy
   blot out my transgressions.
2Wash me thoroughly from my iniquity,
   and cleanse me from my sin!
3For I know my transgressions,
   and my sin is ever before me.
4Against You, You only, have I sinned
   and done what is evil in Your sight,
so that You may be justified in Your words
   and blameless in Your judgment.
5Behold, I was brought forth in iniquity,
   and in sin did my mother conceive me.
6Behold, You delight in truth in the inward being,
   and You teach me wisdom in the secret heart.
7Purge me with hyssop, and I shall be clean;
   wash me, and I shall be whiter than snow.
8Let me hear joy and gladness;
   let the bones that You have broken rejoice.

⁹Hide Your face from my sins,
   and blot out all my iniquities.
¹⁰Create in me a clean heart, O God,
   and renew a right spirit within me.
"Cast me not away from Your presence,
   and take not Your Holy Spirit from me.
¹²Restore to me the joy of Your salvation,
   and uphold me with a willing spirit.
¹³Then I will teach transgressors Your ways,
   and sinners will return to You.
¹⁴Deliver me from bloodguiltiness, O God,
   O God of my salvation,
   and my tongue will sing aloud of Your
                  righteousness.
¹⁵O Lord, open my lips,
   and my mouth will declare your praise.
¹⁶For You will not delight in sacrifice,
      or I would give it;
   You will not be pleased with a burnt offering.
¹⁷The sacrifices of God are a broken spirit;
   a broken and contrite heart, O God,
            You will not despise.
¹⁸Do good to Zion in Your good pleasure;
   build up the walls of Jerusalem;
¹⁹then will You delight in right sacrifices,
   in burnt offerings and whole burnt offerings;
   then bulls will be offered on Your altar.

Consolation and Comfort

Lord, You have been our dwelling place
  in all generations.
²Before the mountains were brought forth,
  or ever You had formed the earth and the world,
  from everlasting to everlasting You are God.
³You return man to dust
  and say, "Return, O children of man!"
⁴For a thousand years in Your sight
  are but as yesterday when it is past,
  or as a watch in the night.
⁵You sweep them away as with a flood;
        they are like a dream,
  like grass that is renewed in the morning:
⁶in the morning it flourishes and is renewed;
  in the evening it fades and withers.
⁷For we are brought to an end by Your anger;
  by Your wrath we are dismayed.
⁸You have set our iniquities before You,
  our secret sins in the light of Your presence.
⁹For all our days pass away under Your wrath;
  we bring our years to an end like a sigh.
¹⁰The years of our life are seventy,
  or even by reason of strength eighty;
yet their span is but toil and trouble;
  they are soon gone, and we fly away.
¹¹Who considers the power of Your anger,
  and Your wrath according to the fear of You?
¹²So teach us to number our days
  that we may get a heart of wisdom.

¹³Return, O LORD! How long?
　　Have pity on Your servants!
¹⁴Satisfy us in the morning with Your steadfast love,
　　that we may rejoice and be glad all our days.
¹⁵Make us glad for as many days as You have
　　　　afflicted us,
　　and for as many years as we have seen evil.
¹⁶Let Your work be shown to Your servants,
　　and Your glorious power to their children.
¹⁷Let the favor of the Lord our God be upon us,
　　and establish the work of our hands upon us;
　　yes, establish the work of our hands!

Morning

Psalm 100

Make a joyful noise to the LORD, all the earth!
　　²Serve the LORD with gladness!
　　Come into His presence with singing!
³Know that the LORD, He is God!
　　It is He who made us, and we are His;
　　we are His people, and the sheep of His pasture.
⁴Enter His gates with thanksgiving,
　　and His courts with praise!
　　Give thanks to Him; bless His name!
⁵For the LORD is good;
　　His steadfast love endures forever,
　　and His faithfulness to all generations.

In Times of Trouble *Psalm 102*

Hear my prayer, O LORD;
let my cry come to You!
²Do not hide Your face from me
   in the day of my distress!
Incline Your ear to me;
   answer me speedily in the day when I call!
³For my days pass away like smoke,
   and my bones burn like a furnace.
⁴My heart is struck down like grass
      and has withered;
   I forget to eat my bread.
⁵Because of my loud groaning
   my bones cling to my flesh.
⁶I am like a desert owl of the wilderness,
   like an owl of the waste places;
⁷I lie awake;
   I am like a lonely sparrow on the housetop.
⁸All the day my enemies taunt me;
   those who deride me use my name for a curse.
⁹For I eat ashes like bread
   and mingle tears with my drink,
¹⁰because of Your indignation and anger;
   for You have taken me up and thrown me down.
¹¹My days are like an evening shadow;
   I wither away like grass.
¹²But You, O LORD, are enthroned forever;
   You are remembered throughout all
      generations.
¹³You will arise and have pity on Zion;

it is the time to favor her;
the appointed time has come.
¹⁴For Your servants hold her stones dear
and have pity on her dust.
¹⁵Nations will fear the name of the LORD,
and all the kings of the earth will fear Your glory.
¹⁶For the LORD builds up Zion;
He appears in His glory;
¹⁷He regards the prayer of the destitute
and does not despise their prayer.
¹⁸Let this be recorded for a generation to come,
so that a people yet to be created may praise
the LORD:
¹⁹that He looked down from His holy height;
from heaven the LORD looked at the earth,
²⁰to hear the groans of the prisoners,
to set free those who were doomed to die,
²¹that they may declare in Zion the name
of the LORD,
and in Jerusalem His praise,
²²when peoples gather together,
and kingdoms, to worship the LORD.
²³He has broken my strength in midcourse;
He has shortened my days.
²⁴"O my God," I say, "take me not away
in the midst of my days—
You whose years endure
throughout all generations!"
²⁵Of old You laid the foundation of the earth,
and the heavens are the work of Your hands.
²⁶They will perish, but You will remain;

they will all wear out like a garment.
You will change them like a robe,
    and they will pass away,
  27but You are the same, and Your years have
        no end.
28The children of Your servants shall dwell secure;
    their offspring shall be established before You.

Assurance

Psalm 119:9–16

How can a young man keep his way pure?
    By guarding it according to Your Word.
10With my whole heart I seek You;
    let me not wander from Your commandments!
11I have stored up Your Word in my heart,
    that I might not sin against You.
12Blessed are You, O LORD;
    teach me Your statutes!
13With my lips I declare
    all the rules of Your mouth.
14In the way of Your testimonies I delight
    as much as in all riches.
15I will meditate on Your precepts
    and fix my eyes on Your ways.
16I will delight in Your statutes;
    I will not forget Your Word.

Forgiveness

Teach me, O LORD, the way of Your statutes;
  and I will keep it to the end.
³⁴Give me understanding, that I may keep Your law
  and observe it with my whole heart.
³⁵Lead me in the path of Your commandments,
  for I delight in it.
³⁶Incline my heart to Your testimonies,
  and not to selfish gain!
³⁷Turn my eyes from looking at worthless things;
  and give me life in Your ways.
³⁸Confirm to Your servant Your promise,
  that You may be feared.
³⁹Turn away the reproach that I dread,
  for Your rules are good.
⁴⁰Behold, I long for Your precepts;
  in your righteousness give me life!
⁴¹Let Your steadfast love come to me, O LORD,
  Your salvation according to Your promise;
⁴²then shall I have an answer for him who taunts me,
  for I trust in Your Word.
⁴³And take not the word of truth utterly out of
      my mouth,
  for my hope is in Your rules.
⁴⁴I will keep Your law continually,
  forever and ever,
⁴⁵and I shall walk in a wide place,
  for I have sought Your precepts.
⁴⁶I will also speak of Your testimonies before kings
  and shall not be put to shame.

Assurance Psalm 121

I lift up my eyes to the hills.
　　From where does my help come?
²My help comes from the LORD,
　　who made heaven and earth.
³He will not let your foot be moved;
　　He who keeps you will not slumber.
⁴Behold, He who keeps Israel
　　will neither slumber nor sleep.
⁵The LORD is your keeper;
　　the LORD is your shade on your right hand.
⁶The sun shall not strike you by day,
　　nor the moon by night.
⁷The LORD will keep you from all evil;
　　He will keep your life.
⁸The LORD will keep
　　your going out and your coming in
　　from this time forth and forevermore.

Marriage Psalm 127

Unless the LORD builds the house,
　　those who build it labor in vain.
Unless the LORD watches over the city,
　　the watchman stays awake in vain.
²It is in vain that you rise up early
　　and go late to rest,
eating the bread of anxious toil;
　　for He gives to His beloved sleep.

³Behold, children are a heritage from the LORD,
   the fruit of the womb a reward.
⁴Like arrows in the hand of a warrior
   are the children of one's youth.
⁵Blessed is the man
   who fills his quiver with them!
He shall not be put to shame
   when he speaks with his enemies in the gate.

Trust in God's Mercy   *Psalm 130:1–6*

Out of the depths I cry to you, O LORD!
   ²O LORD, hear my voice!
Let Your ears be attentive
   to the voice of my pleas for mercy!
³If You, O LORD, should mark iniquities,
   O LORD, who could stand?
⁴But with You there is forgiveness,
   that You may be feared.
⁵I wait for the LORD, my soul waits,
   and in His Word I hope;
⁶my soul waits for the Lord
   more than watchmen for the morning,
   more than watchmen for the morning.

Mealtime, Returning Thanks   *Psalm 136:1, 25*

¹Give thanks to the LORD, for He is good,
    for His steadfast love endures forever.
²⁵He gives food to all flesh,
    for His steadfast love endures forever.

Praise   *Psalm 138*

I give You thanks, O LORD, with my whole heart;
    before the gods I sing Your praise;
²I bow down toward Your holy temple
    and give thanks to Your name for Your steadfast
                love and Your faithfulness,
    for You have exalted above all things
    Your name and Your Word.
³On the day I called, You answered me;
    my strength of soul You increased.
⁴All the kings of the earth shall give You thanks,
        O LORD,
    for they have heard the words of Your mouth,
⁵and they shall sing of the ways of the LORD,
    for great is the glory of the LORD.
⁶For though the LORD is high, He regards the lowly,
    but the haughty He knows from afar.
⁷Though I walk in the midst of trouble,
    You preserve my life;
You stretch out Your hand against the wrath of
        my enemies,
    and Your right hand delivers me.

⁸The LORD will fulfill His purpose for me;
>   Your steadfast love, O LORD, endures forever.
>   Do not forsake the work of Your hands.

Mercy   *Psalm 142*

With my voice I cry out to the LORD;
>   with my voice I plead for mercy to the LORD.
²I pour out my complaint before Him;
>   I tell my trouble before Him.
³When my spirit faints within me,
>   You know my way!
In the path where I walk
>   they have hidden a trap for me.
⁴Look to the right and see:
>   there is none who takes notice of me;
no refuge remains to me;
>   no one cares for my soul.
⁵I cry to you, O LORD;
>   I say, "You are my refuge,
>   my portion in the land of the living."
⁶Attend to my cry,
>   for I am brought very low!
Deliver me from my persecutors,
>   for they are too strong for me!
⁷Bring me out of prison,
>   that I may give thanks to Your name!
The righteous will surround me,
>   for You will deal bountifully with me.

In Time of Danger

Hear my prayer, O LORD;
    give ear to my pleas for mercy!
In Your faithfulness answer me, in Your
        righteousness!
  ²Enter not into judgment with Your servant,
for no one living is righteous before You.
³For the enemy has pursued my soul;
    he has crushed my life to the ground;
    he has made me sit in darkness like those
        long dead.
⁴Therefore my spirit faints within me;
    my heart within me is appalled.
⁵I remember the days of old;
    I meditate on all that You have done;
    I ponder the work of Your hands.
⁶I stretch out my hands to You;
    my soul thirsts for You like a parched land. *Selah*
⁷Answer me quickly, O LORD!
    My spirit fails!
Hide not Your face from me,
    lest I be like those who go down to the pit.
⁸Let me hear in the morning of Your steadfast love,
    for in You I trust.
Make me know the way I should go,
    for to You I lift up my soul.
⁹Deliver me from my enemies, O LORD!
    I have fled to You for refuge!
¹⁰Teach me to do Your will,
    for You are my God!

Let Your good Spirit lead me
    on level ground!
[11]For Your name's sake, O LORD, preserve my life!
    In Your righteousness bring my soul out of trouble!
[12]And in Your steadfast love You will cut off
        my enemies,
    and You will destroy all the adversaries
             of my soul,
    for I am Your servant.

> In the forgiving Word of God the
> incomprehensible greatness of
> God, the intolerable glory of His
> Godhead, the glory of His grace,
> has appeared, has appeared to eyes
> that cannot comprehend it even as
> they gaze upon it. Forgiveness
> remains the perpetual miracle still.
>   — Martin Franzmann[27]

Can I Be Myself?

In moments of honest reflection everyone thinks of some change he would like to make in himself, his attitude, or his abilities. Sometimes such personal evaluation is avoided, consciously or unconsciously. It takes courage to face oneself and to observe the liabilities as well as the assets one may have. An unbalanced view can lead to conceit or to despair, both forms of discontent.

A Christian student surrounded by the pressures of academic competition and social whirl faces such situations where he or she despairs over his or her status. "Why wasn't I made better looking?" "Why can't I get good grades as easily as Jim, who hardly studies?" "Why didn't he ask me out for a second date?" These are but a sampling of the anxieties common in the college world.

Being intimately connected with a loving Savior gives one the courage to look at oneself "in a mirror." The Christian is covered by the blessed righteousness of Christ, which is exceedingly meaningful when a person faces his shortcomings. The Christian knows that God, for the sake of the death and resurrection of Jesus Christ, has accepted him as he is. Such acceptance by God leads to acceptance by oneself. "I can be myself!"

With such liberating acceptance the Christian student sees that changes can be made because he has freedom to grow. Rather than be pressured into changing like "an organization man," the Christian can grow spontaneously as the Holy Spirit enriches his beautiful God-given faith. The Christian student can recognize strengths and shortcomings and use them effectively.

Such accepting faith has another benefit—others are also accepted as they are in a spirit of love. One sees the strengths of another person as a creature of God. Others are objects of God's love too. One can thus cease to be resentful because another appears to be smarter, better looking, or to have some other advantage. Fear, resentment, spiteful competition belongs to the past. "Therefore, if anyone is in Christ, he is a new creation. The old has passed away; behold, the new has come. All this is from God, who through Christ reconciled us to Himself and gave us the ministry of reconciliation" (2 Corinthians 5:17–18).[28]

Rejoice, my heart, be glad and sing,
A cheerful trust maintain;
For God, the source of ev'rything,
Your portion shall remain.

He is your treasure, he your joy,
Your life and light and Lord,
Your counselor when doubts annoy,
Your shield and great reward.

Why spend the day in blank despair,
In restless thought the night?
On your creator cast your care;
He makes your burdens light.

Did not his love and truth and pow'r
Guard ev'ry childhood day?
And did he not in threat'ning hour
Turn dreaded ills away?

He only will with patience chide,
His rod falls gently down,
And all your sins he casts aside;
In ocean depth they drown.

His wisdom never plans in vain
Nor falters nor mistakes
All that his counsels may ordain
A blessed ending makes.

Upon your lips, then, lay your hand
And trust his guiding love;
Then like a rock your peace shall stand
Here and in heav'n above. (*LW* 424)

Text: Paul Gerhardt

Selection of Scripture Lessons

The selection of Scripture Lessons are arranged according to their order in the Bible.

SUGGESTED FOR DEVOTIONAL READING:

—Morning—

Colossians 3:1–4; Exodus 15:1–11; Isaiah 12:1–6;
Matthew 20:1–16; Mark 13:32–36; Luke 24:1–8;
John 21:4–14; Ephesians 4:17–24; Romans 6:1–4.

—Noon—

1 Corinthians 7:17a, 23–24; Luke 23:44–46;
Matthew 5:13–16; Matthew 13:1–9, 18–23;
Mark 13:23–27; John 15:1–9; Romans 7:18–25;
Romans 12:1–2; 1 Peter 1:3–9.

—Early Evening—

Luke 24:28–31; Exodus 16:11–21, 31; Isaiah 25:6–9;
Matthew 14:15–21; Matthew 27:57–60;
Luke 14:15–24; John 6:25–35; John 10:7–18;
Ephesians 6:10–18.

—Close of Day—

Matthew 11:28–30; Micah 7:18–20;
Matthew 18:15–35; Matthew 25:1–13;
Luke 11:1–13; Luke 12:13–34; Romans 8:31–39;
2 Corinthians 4:16–18; Revelation 21:22–22:5.

Then Moses and the people of Israel sang this song
 to the LORD, saying,
"I will sing to the LORD, for He has triumphed
 gloriously;
the horse and his rider He has thrown into the sea.
The LORD is my strength and my song,
 and He has become my salvation;
this is my God, and I will praise Him,
my father's God, and I will exalt Him.
The LORD is a man of war;
the LORD is His name.
"Pharaoh's chariots and his host He cast into the sea,
and his chosen officers were sunk in the Red Sea.
The floods covered them;
they went down into the depths like a stone.
Your right hand, O LORD, glorious in power,
Your right hand, O LORD, shatters the enemy
In the greatness of Your majesty You overthrow
 Your adversaries;
You send out Your fury; it consumes them like stub-
 ble.
At the blast of Your nostrils the waters piled up;
the floods stood up in a heap;
the deeps congealed in the heart of the sea.
The enemy said, 'I will pursue, I will overtake,
I will divide the spoil, my desire shall have its fill of
 them.
I will draw my sword; my hand shall destroy them.'
You blew with Your wind; the sea covered them;

they sank like lead in the mighty waters.
"Who is like You, O LORD, among the gods?
Who is like You, majestic in holiness,
awesome in glorious deeds, doing wonders?"

Early Evening   *Exodus 16:11–21, 31*

And the LORD said to Moses, "I have heard the grumbling of the people of Israel. Say to them, 'At twilight you shall eat meat, and in the morning you shall be filled with bread. Then you shall know that I am the LORD your God.'"

In the evening quail came up and covered the camp, and in the morning dew lay around the camp. And when the dew had gone up, there was on the face of the wilderness a fine, flake-like thing, fine as frost on the ground. When the people of Israel saw it, they said to one another, "What is it?" For they did not know what it was. And Moses said to them, "It is the bread that the LORD has given you to eat. This is what the LORD has commanded: 'Gather of it, each one of you, as much as he can eat. You shall each take an omer, according to the number of the persons that each of you has in his tent.'" And the people of Israel did so. They gathered, some more, some less. But when they measured it with an omer, whoever gathered much had nothing left over, and whoever gathered little had no lack. Each of them gathered as much as he could eat. And Moses said to them, "Let no one leave any of it over till the morning." But they did not listen to Moses. Some left part of it till the morning, and it bred worms and stank. And Moses was angry with them. Morning by morning they gathered it, each as much as he could eat; but when the sun grew hot, it melted. Now the house of Israel called its name manna. It was like coriander seed, white, and the taste of it was like wafers made with honey.

Morning   *Isaiah 12:1–6*

You will say in that day:
"I will give thanks to You, O LORD,
   for though You were angry with me,
Your anger turned away,
   that You might comfort me.
"Behold, God is my salvation;
   I will trust, and will not be afraid;
for the LORD GOD is my strength and my song,
   and He has become my salvation."
   With joy you will draw water from the wells
      of salvation.
And you will say in that day:
"Give thanks to the LORD, call upon His name,
make known His deeds among the peoples,
   proclaim that His name is exalted.
"Sing praises to the LORD, for He has done gloriously;
   let this be made known in all the earth.
Shout, and sing for joy, O inhabitant of Zion,
   for great in your midst is the Holy One of Israel."

On this mountain the LORD of hosts will make for
      all peoples
a feast of rich food, a feast of well-aged wine,
of rich food full of marrow, of aged wine well refined.
    And He will swallow up on this mountain
the covering that is cast over all peoples,
the veil that is spread over all nations.
    He will swallow up death forever;
and the LORD GOD will wipe away tears from
      all faces,
and the reproach of His people He will take away
      from all the earth,
for the LORD has spoken.
    It will be said on that day,
"Behold, this is our God; we have waited for Him,
      that He might save us.
This is the LORD; we have waited for Him;
let us be glad and rejoice in His salvation.

> We are so used to thinking of body
> and soul, flesh and spirit, as opposites
> that we no longer understand that the
> whole magnitude of God's love lies in
> this very fact. God's Son comes to us
> in the flesh and the Holy Spirit binds
> Himself to the external means of grace.
> —Hermann Sasse[29]

Close of Day
Micah 7:18–20

Who is a God like You, pardoning iniquity and passing over transgression for the remnant of His inheritance?

He does not retain His anger forever, because He delights in steadfast love.

He will again have compassion on us; He will tread our iniquities under foot.

You will cast all our sins into the depths of the sea.

You will show faithfulness to Jacob and steadfast love to Abraham,

as You have sworn to our fathers from the days of old.

Noon
Matthew 5:13–16

[Jesus spoke to them saying,] "You are the salt of the earth, but if salt has lost its taste, how shall its saltiness be restored? It is no longer good for anything except to be thrown out and trampled under people's feet.

"You are the light of the world. A city set on a hill cannot be hidden. Nor do people light a lamp and put it under a basket, but on a stand, and it gives light to all in the house. In the same way, let your light shine before others, so that they may see your good works and give glory to your Father who is in heaven."

Close of Day   *Matthew 11:28–30*

[Jesus said,] "Come to Me, all who labor and are heavy laden, and I will give you rest. Take My yoke upon you, and learn from Me, for I am gentle and lowly in heart, and you will find rest for your souls. For My yoke is easy, and My burden is light."

Noon   *Matthew 13:1–9, 18–23*

That same day Jesus went out of the house and sat beside the sea. And great crowds gathered about Him, so that He got into a boat and sat down. And the whole crowd stood on the beach. And He told them many things in parables, saying: "A sower went out to sow. And as he sowed, some seeds fell along the path, and the birds came and devoured them. Other seeds fell on rocky ground, where they did not have much soil, and immediately they sprang up, since they had no depth of soil, but when the sun rose they were scorched. And since they had no root, they withered away. Other seeds fell among thorns, and the thorns grew up and choked them. Other seeds fell on good soil and produced grain, some a hundredfold, some sixty, some thirty. He who has ears, let him hear.

"Hear then the parable of the sower: When anyone hears the word of the kingdom and does not understand it, the evil one comes and snatches away what has been sown in his heart. This is what was sown along the path. As for what was sown on rocky ground, this is the one who hears the word and immediately receives it with joy, yet he has no root in himself, but endures for a while, and when tribulation or persecution arises on account of the word, immediately he falls away. As for what was sown among thorns, this is the one who hears the word, but the cares of the world and the deceitfulness of riches choke the word, and it proves unfruitful. As for what was sown on good soil, this is the one who hears the word and understands it. He indeed bears fruit and yields, in one case a hundredfold, in another sixty, and in another thirty.

Early Evening   *Matthew 14:15–21*

Now when it was evening, the disciples came to [Jesus] and said, "This is a desolate place, and the day is now over; send the crowds away to go into the villages and buy food for themselves." But Jesus said, "They need not go away; you give them something to eat." They said to Him, "We have only five loaves here and two fish." And He said, "Bring them here to Me." Then He ordered the crowds to sit down on the grass, and taking the five loaves and the two fish, He looked up to heaven and said a blessing. Then He broke the loaves and gave them to the disciples, and the disciples gave them to the crowds. And they all ate and were satisfied. And they took up twelve baskets full of the broken pieces left over. And those who ate were about five thousand men, besides women and children.

Close of Day   *Matthew 18:15–35*

[Jesus said to them] "If your brother sins against you, go and tell him his fault, between you and him alone. If he listens to you, you have gained your brother. But if he does not listen, take one or two others along with you, that every charge may be established by the evidence of two or three witnesses. If he refuses to listen to them, tell it to the church. And if he refuses to listen even to the church, let him be to you as a Gentile and a tax collector. Truly, I say to you, whatever you bind on earth shall be bound in heaven, and whatever you loose on earth shall be loosed in heaven. Again I say to you, if two of you agree on earth about anything they ask, it will be done for them by My Father in heaven. For where two or three are gathered in My name, there am I among them."

Then Peter came up and said to Him, "Lord, how often will my brother sin against me, and I forgive him? As many as seven times?" Jesus said to him, "I do not say to you seven times, but seventy times seven.

"Therefore the kingdom of heaven may be compared to a king who wished to settle accounts with his servants. When he began to settle, one was brought to him who owed him ten thousand talents. And since he could not pay, his master ordered him to be sold, with his wife and children and all that he had, and payment to be made. So the servant fell on his knees, imploring him, 'Have patience with me, and I will pay you everything.' And out of pity for him, the master of that servant released him and forgave him the debt. But when that same servant went out, he found one of his fellow servants who owed him a hundred denarii, and seizing him, he began to choke him, saying, 'Pay what you owe.' So his fellow servant fell down and pleaded with him, 'Have patience with me, and I will pay you.' He refused and went and put him in prison until he should pay the debt. When his fellow servants saw what had taken place, they were greatly distressed, and they went and reported to their master all that had taken place. Then his master summoned him and said to him, 'You wicked servant! I forgave you all that debt because you pleaded with me. And should not you have had mercy on your fellow servant, as I had mercy on you?' And in anger his master delivered him to the jailers, until he should pay all his debt. So also My heavenly Father will do to every one of you, if you do not forgive your brother from your heart."

[Jesus told them this parable,] "For the kingdom of heaven is like a master of a house who went out early in the morning to hire laborers for his vineyard. After agreeing with the laborers for a denarius a day, he sent them into his vineyard. And going out about the third hour he saw others standing idle in the marketplace, and to them he said, 'You go into the vineyard too, and whatever is right I will give you.' So they went. Going out again about the sixth hour and the ninth hour, he did the same. And about the eleventh hour he went out and found others standing. And he said to them, 'Why do you stand here idle all day?' They said to him, 'Because no one has hired us.' He said to them, 'You go into the vineyard too.' And when evening came, the owner of the vineyard said to his foreman, 'Call the laborers and pay them their wages, beginning with the last, up to the first.' And when those hired about the eleventh hour came, each of them received a denarius. Now when those hired first came, they thought they would receive more, but each of them also received a denarius. And on receiving it they grumbled at the master of the house, saying, 'These last worked only one hour, and you have made them equal to us who have borne the burden of the day and the scorching heat.' But he replied to one of them, 'Friend, I am doing you no wrong. Did you not agree with me for a denarius?

Take what belongs to you and go. I choose to give to this last worker as I give to you. Am I not allowed to do what I choose with what belongs to me? Or do you begrudge my generosity?' So the last will be first, and the first last."

Close of Day   *Matthew 25:1–13*

[Jesus told them this parable,]"Then the kingdom of heaven will be like ten virgins who took their lamps and went to meet the bridegroom. Five of them were foolish, and five were wise. For when the foolish took their lamps, they took no oil with them, but the wise took flasks of oil with their lamps. As the bridegroom was delayed, they all became drowsy and slept. But at midnight there was a cry, 'Here is the bridegroom! Come out to meet him.' Then all those virgins rose and trimmed their lamps. And the foolish said to the wise, 'Give us some of your oil, for our lamps are going out.' But the wise answered, saying, 'Since there will not be enough for us and for you, go rather to the dealers and buy for yourselves.' And while they were going to buy, the bridegroom came, and those who were ready went in with him to the marriage feast, and the door was shut. Afterward the other virgins came also, saying, 'Lord, lord, open to us.' But he answered, 'Truly, I say to you, I do not know you.' Watch therefore, for you know neither the day nor the hour."

Early Evening   *Matthew 27:57–60*

When it was evening, there came a rich man from Arimathea, named Joseph, who also was a disciple of Jesus. He went to Pilate and asked for the body of Jesus. Then Pilate ordered it to be given to him. And Joseph took the body and wrapped it in a clean linen shroud and laid it in his own new tomb, which he had cut in the rock. And he rolled a great stone to the entrance of the tomb and went away.

Noon   *Mark 13:23–27*

[Jesus spoke to them saying,] "But be on guard; I have told you all things beforehand. But in those days, after that tribulation, the sun will be darkened, and the moon will not give its light, and the stars will be falling from heaven, and the powers in the heavens will be shaken. And then will see the Son of Man coming in clouds with great power and glory. And then He will send out the angels and gather His elect from the four winds, from the ends of the earth to the ends of heaven."

Morning

[Jesus spoke to them saying,] "But concerning that day or that hour, no one knows, not even the angels in heaven, nor the Son, but only the Father. Be on guard, keep awake. For you do not know when the time will come. It is like a man going on a journey, when he leaves home and puts his servants in charge, each with his work, and commands the doorkeeper to stay awake. Therefore stay awake—for you do not know when the master of the house will come, in the evening, or at midnight, or when the cock crows, or in the morning—lest he come suddenly and find you asleep. And what I say to you I say to all: Stay awake."

Close of Day

Now Jesus was praying in a certain place, and when He finished, one of His disciples said to Him, "Lord, teach us to pray, as John taught his disciples." And He said to them,

> "When you pray, say:
> "Father, hallowed be Your name.
> Your kingdom come.
> Give us each day our daily bread,
> and forgive us our sins,
> as we forgive everyone who
> [sins against] us.
> And lead us not into temptation."

And He said to them, "Which of you who has a friend will go to him at midnight and say to him, 'Friend, lend me three loaves, for a friend of mine has arrived on a journey, and I have nothing to set before him'; and he will answer from within, 'Do not bother me; the door is now shut, and my children are with me in bed. I cannot get up and give you anything'? I tell you, though he will not get up and give him anything because he is his friend, yet because of his impudence he will rise and give him whatever he needs. And I tell you, ask, and it will be given to you; seek, and you will find; knock, and it will be opened to you. For everyone who asks receives, and the one who seeks finds, and to the one who knocks it will be opened. What father among you, if his son asks for a fish, will instead of a fish give him a serpent; or if he asks for an egg, will give him a scorpion? If you then, who are evil, know how to give good gifts to your children, how much more will the heavenly Father give the Holy Spirit to those who ask Him!"

Close of Day   *Luke 12:13–34*

Someone in the crowd said to [Jesus], "Teacher, tell my brother to divide the inheritance with me." But He said to him, "Man, who made me a judge or arbitrator over you?" And He said to them, "Take care, and be on your guard against all covetousness, for one's life does not consist in the abundance of his possessions." And He told them a parable, saying, "The land of a rich man produced plentifully, and he thought to himself, 'What shall I do, for I have nowhere to store my crops?' And he said, 'I will do this: I will tear down my barns and build larger ones, and there I will store all my grain and my goods. And I will say to my soul, Soul, you have ample goods laid up for many years; relax, eat, drink, be merry.' But God said to him, 'Fool! This night your soul is required of you, and the things you have prepared, whose will they be?' So is the one who lays up treasure for himself and is not rich toward God."

And He said to His disciples, "Therefore I tell you, do not be anxious about your life, what you will eat, nor about your body, what you will put on. For life is more than food, and the body more than clothing. Consider the ravens: they neither sow nor reap, they have neither storehouse nor barn, and yet God feeds them. Of how much more value are you than the birds! And which of you by being anxious can add a single hour to his span of life? If then you are not able to do as small a thing as that, why are you anxious about the rest? Consider the lilies, how they grow: they neither toil nor spin, yet I tell you, even Solomon in all his glory was not arrayed like one of these. But if God so clothes the grass, which is alive in the field today, and tomorrow is thrown into the oven, how much more will He clothe you, O you of little faith! And do not seek what you are tò eat and what you are to drink, nor be worried. For all the nations of the world seek after these things, and your Father knows that you need them. Instead, seek His kingdom, and these things will be added to you.

"Fear not, little flock, for it is your Father's good pleasure to give you the kingdom. Sell your possessions, and give to the needy. Provide yourselves with moneybags that do not grow old, with a treasure in the heavens that does not fail, where no thief approaches and no moth destroys. For where your treasure is, there will your heart be also."

Evening Prayer   *Luke 14:15–24*

When one of those who reclined at table with [Jesus] heard these things, He said to him, "Blessed is everyone who will eat bread in the kingdom of God!" But [Jesus] said to him, "A man once gave a great banquet and invited many. And at the time for the banquet he sent his servant to say to those who had been invited, 'Come, for everything is now ready.' But they all alike began to make excuses. The first said to him, 'I have bought a field, and I must go out and see it. Please have me excused.' And another said, 'I have bought five yoke of oxen, and I go to examine them. Please have me excused.' And another said, 'I have married a wife, and therefore I cannot come.' So the servant came and reported these things to his master. Then the master of the house became angry and said to his servant, 'Go out quickly to the streets and lanes of the city, and bring in the poor and crippled and blind and lame.' And the servant said, 'Sir, what you commanded has been done, and still there is room.' And the master said to the servant, 'Go out to the highways and hedges and compel people to come in, that my house may be filled. For I tell you, none of those men who were invited shall taste my banquet.' "

Noon Prayer   *Luke 23:44–46*

It was now about the sixth hour, and there was darkness over the whole land until the ninth hour, while the sun's light failed. And the curtain of the temple was torn in two. Then Jesus, calling out with a loud voice, said, "Father, into Your hands I commit My spirit!" And having said this He breathed his last.

Morning   *Luke 24:1–8*

But on the first day of the week, at early dawn, they went to [Jesus'] tomb, taking the spices they had prepared. And they found the stone rolled away from the tomb, but when they went in they did not find the body of the Lord Jesus. While they were perplexed about this, behold, two men stood by them in dazzling apparel. And as they were frightened and bowed their faces to the ground, the men said to them, "Why do you seek the living among the dead? He is not here, but has risen. Remember how He told you, while He was still in Galilee, that the Son of Man must be delivered into the hands of sinful men and be crucified and on the third day rise." And they remembered His words.

"It is understandable that for the modern man, just like the rational man of the ancient world, the accounts of the New Testament elicit no faith, and that he asserts that they are legends, mythology, or deception. But there is no justification for us to make of the New Testament Easter message something other than it is. Faith in the Risen One is faith in the one who truly rose from the dead and actually appeared to His disciples, who did not remain in the grave, but rose as the firstfruits from the dead."

—Sasse[32]

Early Evening   *Luke 24:28–31*

So they drew near to the village to which they were going. [The Lord] acted as if He were going farther, but they urged Him strongly, saying, "Stay with us, for it is toward evening and the day is now far spent." So He went in to stay with them. When He was at table with them, He took the bread and blessed and broke it and gave it to them. And their eyes were opened, and they recognized Him. And He vanished from their sight.

When they found Him on the other side of the sea, they said to Him, "Rabbi, when did You come here?" Jesus answered them, "Truly, truly, I say to you, you are seeking Me, not because you saw signs, but because you ate your fill of the loaves. Do not labor for the food that perishes, but for the food that endures to eternal life, which the Son of Man will give to you. For on Him God the Father has set His seal." Then they said to Him, "What must we do, to be doing the works of God?" Jesus answered them, "This is the work of God, that you believe in Him whom He has sent." So they said to Him, "Then what sign do you do, that we may see and believe You? What work do You perform? Our fathers ate the manna in the wilderness; as it is written, 'He gave them bread from heaven to eat.'" Jesus then said to them, "Truly, truly, I say to you, it was not Moses who gave you the bread from heaven, but My Father gives you the true bread from heaven. For the bread of God is He who comes down from heaven and gives life to the world." They said to Him, "Sir, give us this bread always."

Jesus said to them, "I am the bread of life; whoever comes to Me shall not hunger, and whoever believes in Me shall never thirst."

Early Evening

So Jesus again said to them, "Truly, truly, I say to you, I am the door of the sheep. All who came before Me are thieves and robbers, but the sheep did not listen to them. I am the door. If anyone enters by Me, he will be saved and will go in and out and find pasture. The thief comes only to steal and kill and destroy. I came that they may have life and have it abundantly. I am the good shepherd. The good shepherd lays down his life for the sheep. He who is a hired hand and not a shepherd, who does not own the sheep, sees the wolf coming and leaves the sheep and flees, and the wolf snatches them and scatters them. He flees because he is a hired hand and cares nothing for the sheep. I am the good shepherd. I know My own and My own know Me, just as the Father knows Me and I know the Father; and I lay down My life for the sheep. And I have other sheep that are not of this fold. I must bring them also, and they will listen to My voice. So there will be one flock, one shepherd. For this reason the Father loves Me, because I lay down My life that I may take it up again. No one takes it from Me, but I lay it down of My own accord. I have authority to lay it down, and I have authority to take it up again. This charge I have received from My Father."

Noon John 15:1–9

[Jesus spoke to them saying,] "I am the true vine, and My Father is the vinedresser. Every branch of Mine that does not bear fruit He takes away, and every branch that does bear fruit He prunes, that it may bear more fruit. Already you are clean because of the word that I have spoken to you. Abide in Me, and I in you. As the branch cannot bear fruit by itself, unless it abides in the vine, neither can you, unless you abide in me. I am the vine; you are the branches. Whoever abides in Me and I in him, he it is that bears much fruit, for apart from Me you can do nothing. If anyone does not abide in Me he is thrown away like a branch and withers; and the branches are gathered, thrown into the fire, and burned. If you abide in Me, and My words abide in you, ask whatever you wish, and it will be done for you. By this My Father is glorified, that you bear much fruit and so prove to be My disciples. As the Father has loved Me, so have I loved you. Abide in My love."

Morning John 21:4–14

Just as day was breaking, Jesus stood on the shore; yet the disciples did not know that it was Jesus. Jesus said to them, "Children, do you have any fish?" They answered Him, "No." He said to them, "Cast the net on the right side of the boat,

and you will find some." So they cast it, and now they were not able to haul it in, because of the quantity of fish. That disciple whom Jesus loved therefore said to Peter, "It is the Lord!" When Simon Peter heard that it was the Lord, he put on his outer garment, for he was stripped for work, and threw himself into the sea. The other disciples came in the boat, dragging the net full of fish, for they were not far from the land, but about a hundred yards off.

When they got out on land, they saw a charcoal fire in place, with fish laid out on it, and bread. Jesus said to them, "Bring some of the fish that you have just caught." So Simon Peter went aboard and hauled the net ashore, full of large fish, 153 of them. And although there were so many, the net was not torn. Jesus said to them, "Come and have breakfast." Now none of the disciples dared ask Him, "Who are You?" They knew it was the Lord. Jesus came and took the bread and gave it to them, and so with the fish. This was now the third time that Jesus was revealed to the disciples after He was raised from the dead.

The Christian knows that he must press forward if he is not to fall back, but because his active renewal in Christ is always inadequate he does not find in it the ground nor even the confirmation of his fellowship with God; that he finds in the promises of the Gospel.

—Albert Koberle[31]

Morning   *Romans 6:1–4*

What shall we say then? Are we to continue in sin that grace may abound? By no means! How can we who died to sin still live in it? Do you not know that all of us who have been baptized into Christ Jesus were baptized into His death? We were buried therefore with Him by baptism into death, in order that, just as Christ was raised from the dead by the glory of the Father, we too might walk in newness of life.

Noon   *Romans 7:18–25*

For I know that nothing good dwells in me, that is, in my flesh. For I have the desire to do what is right, but not the ability to carry it out. For I do not do the good I want, but the evil I do not want is what I keep on doing. Now if I do what I do not want, it is no longer I who do it, but sin that dwells within me.

So I find it to be a law that when I want to do right, evil lies close at hand. For I delight in the law of God, in my inner being, but I see in my members another law waging war against the law of my mind and making me captive to the law of sin that dwells in my members. Wretched man that I am! Who will deliver me from this body of death? Thanks be to God through Jesus Christ our Lord! So then, I myself serve the law of God with my mind, but with my flesh I serve the law of sin.

Close of Day *Romans 8:31–39*

What then shall we say to these things? If God is for us, who can be against us? He who did not spare His own Son but gave Him up for us all, how will He not also with Him graciously give us all things? Who shall bring any charge against God's elect? It is God who justifies. Who is to condemn? Christ Jesus is the one who died—more than that, who was raised—who is at the right hand of God, who indeed is interceding for us. Who shall separate us from the love of Christ? Shall tribulation, or distress, or persecution, or famine, or nakedness, or danger, or sword? As it is written,

> "For your sake we are being killed
>   all the day long;
> we are regarded as sheep to be
>   slaughtered."

No, in all these things we are more than conquerors through Him who loved us. For I am sure that neither death nor life, nor angels nor rulers, nor things present nor things to come, nor powers, nor height nor depth, nor anything else in all creation, will be able to separate us from the love of God in Christ Jesus our Lord.

Noon *Romans 12:1–2*

I appeal to you therefore, brothers, by the mercies of God, to present your bodies as a living sacrifice, holy and acceptable to God, which is your spiritual worship. Do not be conformed to this world, but be transformed by the renewal of your mind, that by testing you may discern what is the will of God, what is good and acceptable and perfect.

Noon *1 Corinthians 7:17a, 23–24*

Only let each person lead the life that the Lord has assigned to him, and to which God has called him. You were bought with a price; do not become slaves of men. So, brothers, in whatever condition each was called, there let him remain with God.

Close of Day *2 Corinthians 4:16–18*

So we do not lose heart. Though our outer nature is wasting away, our inner nature is being renewed day by day. For this slight momentary affliction is preparing for us an eternal weight of glory beyond all comparison, as we look not to the things that are seen but to the things that are unseen. For the things that are seen are transient, but the things that are unseen are eternal.

Morning Prayer   *Ephesians 4:17–24*

Now this I say and testify in the Lord, that you must no longer walk as the Gentiles do, in the futility of their minds. They are darkened in their understanding, alienated from the life of God because of the ignorance that is in them, due to their hardness of heart. They have become callous and have given themselves up to sensuality, greedy to practice every kind of impurity. But that is not the way you learned Christ!—assuming that you have heard about Him and were taught in Him, as the truth is in Jesus, to put off your old self, which belongs to your former manner of life and is corrupt through deceitful desires, and to be renewed in the spirit of your minds, and to put on the new self, created after the likeness of God in true righteousness and holiness.

Early Evening   *Ephesians 6:10–18*

Finally, be strong in the Lord and in the strength of His might. Put on the whole armor of God, that you may be able to stand against the schemes of the devil. For we do not wrestle against flesh and blood, but against the rulers, against the authorities, against the cosmic powers over this present darkness, against the spiritual forces of evil in the heavenly places. Therefore take up the whole armor of God, that you may be able to withstand in the evil day, and having done all, to stand firm. Stand therefore, having fastened on the belt of truth, and having put on the breastplate of righteousness, and, as shoes for your feet, having put on the readiness given by the gospel of peace. In all circumstances take up the shield of faith, with which you can extinguish all the flaming darts of the evil one; and take the helmet of salvation, and the sword of the Spirit, which is the word of God, praying at all times in the Spirit, with all prayer and supplication. To that end keep alert with all perseverance, making supplication for all the saints.

Morning   *Colossians 3:1–4*

If then you have been raised with Christ, seek the things that are above, where Christ is seated at the right hand of God. Set your minds on things that are above, not on things that are on earth. For you have died, and your life is hidden with Christ in God. When Christ who is your life appears, then you also will appear with Him in glory.

Blessed be the God and Father of our Lord Jesus Christ! According to His great mercy, He has caused us to be born again to a living hope through the resurrection of Jesus Christ from the dead, to an inheritance that is imperishable, undefiled, and unfading, kept in heaven for you, who by God's power are being guarded through faith for a salvation ready to be revealed in the last time. In this you rejoice, though now for a little while, if necessary, you have been grieved by various trials, so that the tested genuineness of your faith—more precious than gold that perishes though it is tested by fire—may be found to result in praise and glory and honor at the revelation of Jesus Christ. Though you have not seen Him, you love Him. Though you do not now see Him, you believe in Him and rejoice with joy that is inexpressible and filled with glory, obtaining the outcome of your faith, the salvation of your souls.

> We need more than anything else in this world a hunger for God, a stomach-growling, voracious craving for God and the holy things of God. We need to be spiritually hungry. The bread of God gives life to the world. It keeps a person going forever.
> —Harold L. Senkbeil[30]

And I saw no temple in the city, for its temple is the Lord God the Almighty and the Lamb. And the city has no need of sun or moon to shine on it, for the glory of God gives it light, and its lamp is the Lamb. By its light will the nations walk, and the kings of the earth will bring their glory into it, and its gates will never be shut by day—and there will be no night there. They will bring into it the glory and the honor of the nations. But nothing unclean will ever enter it, nor anyone who does what is detestable or false, but only those who are written in the Lamb's book of life.

Then the angel showed me the river of the water of life, bright as crystal, flowing from the throne of God and of the Lamb through the middle of the street of the city; also, on either side of the river, the tree of life with its twelve kinds of fruit, yielding its fruit each month. The leaves of the tree were for the healing of the nations. No longer will there be anything accursed, but the throne of God and of the Lamb will be in it, and His servants will worship Him. They will see His face, and His name will be on their foreheads. And night will be no more. They will need no light of lamp or sun, for the Lord God will be their light, and they will reign forever and ever.

Certainly Jesus is important as a moral Teacher. History places His name among the great, like Socrates, Plato, and Epictetus, with all the great ethical leaders of the past. Just about everyone with little or great education will recognize Jesus of Nazareth as a very fine man who taught high ideals. The English poet Matthew Arnold wrote in his poem The Better Part:

Hath man no second life? Pitch this one high!
Sits there no judge in heaven, our sin to see?
More strictly then the inward judge obey!
Was Christ a man like us? Oh, let us try
If we then, too, can be such men as He!

Jesus is a great moral Teacher, to be sure! But He is more—much more—He is the Savior, whose atoning work of love is the motivation for true ethical living. Christ's teachings apart from His person and apart from His work of redemption are fruits with no roots.

The teachings of Jesus are directives showing how love will act in certain situations, but above all He has first and foremost restored man to fellowship with God. He has accomplished a renewed relationship of divine love between God and man.

Here is the root of the ethics of Jesus. "As I have loved you, love one another," our Lord tells us.

On the campus we are called to confess the basic Saviorhood of Jesus Christ. Our Lord is more to us than merely a great teacher, more than even the best of teachers—He is Lord and Savior. The forgiveness of sins and a right relationship with our Creator are the fountain for meaningful living among our fellow human beings. Love, mercy, understanding, and other Christian virtues are born of a person's knowing his God in Christ, "faith working through love." [32]

God loved the world so that He gave
His only Son the lost to save
That all who would in him believe
Should everlasting life receive.

Christ Jesus is the ground of faith,
Who was made flesh and suffered death;
All who confide in Christ alone
Are built on this chief cornerstone.

Be of good cheer, for God's own Son
Forgives all sins which you have done;
And justified by Jesus' blood,
Baptized, you have the highest good.

Glory to God the Father, Son,
And Holy Spirit, Three in One!
To you, O blessed Trinity,
Be praise now and eternally!
(*LW* 352)

Text: L. Bolhagen, tr. August Crull

It is time for us to use God's Word and prayer and to utilize the church's prayers for the blessing of all who suffer. The gift of God we already have may slumber but it can also be awakened. The Lord has not removed from our church the gift of prayer; he hears and answers its cries. If we use this gift we shall soon realize the help and powerful answer through which the pure Word and the great blessing it brings.

—Wilhelm Loehe[34]

Prayers
for Ourselves and Others

General Prayer

O God almighty and merciful, let Your fatherly kindness be upon all whom You have made; hear the prayers of all who call upon You; open the eyes of those who never pray for themselves; pity the sighs of such as are in misery; deal mercifully with those who are in darkness; increase the number and graces of those who fear and serve You daily; preserve this land from the misfortunes of war, this church from all wild and dangerous errors, this people from forgetting You, their Lord and Benefactor; be gracious to all those countries that are made desolate by earthquakes, droughts, floods, epidemics, or persecution; bless all persons and places to which Your providence has made us debtors, all who have been instrumental to our good by their assistance, advice, example, or writings, and make us in our turn useful to others; let none of those who desire our prayers want for Your mercy, but defend and comfort and conduct them through to their life's end; through Jesus Christ, Your Son, our Lord. Amen. (1)

The Litany

*When used in group settings, the responses are set in **bold type**.*

O Lord, **have mercy**. O Christ, **have mercy**. O Lord, **have mercy**. O Christ, hear us. God the Father, in heaven, **have mercy**. God the Son, Redeemer of the world, **have mercy**. God the Holy Spirit, **have mercy**. Be gracious to us. **Spare us, good Lord**. Be gracious to us. **Help us, good Lord.**

From all sin, from all error, from all evil: from the crafts and assaults of the devil; from sudden and evil death: from pestilence and famine; from war and bloodshed; from sedition and from rebellion: from lightning and **tempest; from all calamity by fire and water; and from everlasting death: Good** Lord, deliver us.

By the mystery of Your holy incarnation; by Your holy nativity: by Your baptism, fasting, and temptation; by Your agony and bloody sweat; by Your cross and Passion; by Your precious death and burial; by Your glorious resurrection and ascension; and by the coming of the Holy Spirit, the Comforter: **Help us, good Lord.**

In all time of our tribulation; in all time of our prosperity; in the hour of death; and in the day of judgment: **Help us, good Lord**. We poor sinners implore You to **hear us, O Lord.**

To rule and govern Your holy Christian Church; to preserve all pastors and ministers of Your Church in the true knowledge and understanding of Your wholesome Word and to sustain them in holy living: to put an end to all schisms and causes of offense; to bring into the way of truth all who have erred and are deceived; to beat down Satan under our feet; to send faithful laborers into Your harvest; and to accompany Your Word with Your grace and Spirit: **We implore You to hear us, good Lord.**

To raise those that fall and to strengthen those that stand; and to comfort and help the weakhearted and the distressed: **We implore You to hear us, good Lord.** To give to all peoples concord and peace; to preserve our land from discord and strife; to give our country Your protection in every time of need; to direct and defend our president and all in authority; to bless and protect our magistrates and all our people; to watch over and help all who are in danger, necessity, and tribulation; to protect and guide all who travel; to grant all women with child, and all mothers with infant children, increasing happiness in their blessings; to defend all orphans and widows and provide for them; to strengthen and keep all sick persons and young children; to free those in bondage; and to have mercy on us all: **We implore You to hear us, good Lord.**

To forgive our enemies, persecutors, and slanderers and to turn their hearts; to give and preserve to our use the kindly fruits of the earth; and graciously to hear our prayers: **We implore You to hear us, good Lord.** Lord Jesus Christ, Son of God, **we implore You to hear us.**

Christ, the Lamb of God, who takes away the sin of the world, **have mercy.** Christ, the Lamb of God, who takes away the sin of the world, **have mercy.** Christ, the Lamb of God, who takes away the sin of the world, **grant us Your peace.** O Christ, **hear us.** O Lord, **have mercy.** O Christ, **have mercy.** O Lord, **have mercy. Amen.** (2)

Confession and Deliverance

Almighty and merciful God, the Fountain of all goodness, who knows the thoughts of my heart, I confess unto You that I have sinned against You and am evil in your sight; wash me, I implore You, from the stains of my past sins, and give me grace and power to put away all hurtful things, so that, being delivered from the bondage of sin, I may bring forth worthy fruits of repentance; O Eternal Light, shine into my heart; O Eternal Goodness, deliver me from evil; O Eternal Power, be to me a support; eternal Wisdom, scatter the darkness of my ignorance; eternal Pity, have mercy upon me; grant unto me that with all my heart and mind and strength I may evermore seek Your face; and finally bring me in Your infinite mercy to Your holy presence; so strengthen my weakness that, following in the footsteps of Your blessed Son, I may obtain the promise of my Baptism and enter into Your promised joy; through the same Jesus Christ, Your Son, our Lord. Amen. (3)

For the Church

O God, our heavenly Father, who manifested Your love by sending Your only-begotten Son into the world that all might live through Him, pour Your Holy Spirit upon Your church that it may fulfill His command to preach the Gospel in every land; send forth, we implore You, laborers into Your harvest; defend them in all dangers and temptations and hasten the time when they and those whom they have brought to You will meet and rejoice before Your heavenly throne; through Jesus Christ, Your Son, our Lord. Amen. (4)

For Those Who Work In Campus Ministry

Lord Jesus, Chief Shepherd of the sheep, I thank You for all who work in Your Word and Sacrament ministry on this campus. By Your grace and mercy keep them faithful and true.

> Keep me grateful to them
> For preaching and teaching Your Word
> in truth;
> For their fellowship in the Gospel;
> For their influence in the community;
> For the example of their Christian life.

May I always be aware of my obligation to pray for my pastor and those who do the work of the church in our midst; to honor them and support them and his ministry among us. Bless our pastor and continue to make him a blessing to me and the work of Your kingdom.

Help my pastor and all those who give their time, talents and treasure to this campus ministry to be steadfast in faith, and, at the last, take us all into the Church Triumphant with You above. In Your name I pray. Amen. (5)

For Profitable Use Of The Word

Dear God! You speak through your dear Son: Blessed are those that hear your Word. How much easier it would be, were we to praise and thank You unceasingly with joyful hearts that you have so benevolently and fatherly revealed yourself to us lowly creatures, speaking to us concerning the greatest and best of all matters, namely, eternal life! At the same time you never stop calling us through your Son's Holy Word: Blessed are those that hear God's Word and keep it. You would never have our ears do without it, and we who are but earth and ashes continuously need your blessed Word! Oh, how unspeakably great and wondrous are your goodness and patience. On the other hand, affliction and woe be upon the thankless-ness and stubborn blindness of those who not only refuse to hear your Word alone, but also treat it with deliberate mockery, persecution and spite. Amen. (6)

Before Communion

Lord Jesus Christ, You call to Yourself all those that labor and are heavy burdened, to refresh them and to give rest to their souls. Dear Lord, I pray, let me also experience Your love at the heavenly feast, which You have prepared for Your children on earth. Keep me from impenitence and unbelief, so that I do not receive the Sacrament to my damnation. Remove the spotted garment of my flesh and my own righteousness, and adorn me with the garment earned by Your blood. Strengthen my faith, increase my love and hope, and hereafter make me to sit at Your heavenly table, where You give me to eat of the eternal manna to drink of the river of Your pleasures. Hear me for Your own sake. Amen. (7)

For Those Who Have Forsaken the Faith

Almighty, merciful, and gracious God and Father, visit those who have forsaken the Christian faith and those who wandered from Your Word; reveal to them their error and bring them back from their wanderings, that they with singleness of heart, and taking pleasure in the pure truth of Your Word alone, may be made partakers of eternal life; through Jesus Christ, Your Son, our Lord. Amen. (8)

For Non-Christian Classmates and Friends

O God of all the nations of the earth, remember the unbelievers who, though created in Your image, are perishing in their sin; and grant that by the prayers and labors of Your holy church they may be delivered from all superstitions and unbelief and brought to worship You; through Him who you have sent to be our Salvation, the Resurrection and the Life of all the faithful, Your Son, Jesus Christ, our Lord. Amen. (9)

Prayer of Luther on Casting All Our Cares upon the Lord

Heavenly Father, You are truly my Lord and my God; You have created me, bringing me out of nothing, and You have redeemed me through Your Son. You have appointed and assigned to me this office—this place in life—and all these duties, but matters do not always take the turn I should like them to take, and there are so many things troubling and distressing me that in myself I find neither hope nor consolation. For this very reason I commit everything to You, looking to You for counsel and aid. In all these questions be the Beginning and the End. Amen. (10)

Beginning a Group Activity or Endeavor

God, You are the Creator, Redeemer, and Sanctifier. We meet You as You come to us in Word and Sacrament, as You come to us in grace and blessing. We thank You for calling us into Your kingdom. We thank You for allowing us to be members of this congregation. We thank You for appointing us as workers with the saints in this church body. We need Your power to work effectively and to overcome the forces of evil that frustrate Your saving intentions. We seek Your grace, to care for people as You do and to endure hostility and misunderstanding in our efforts to help. We ask that Your holiness fill our lives. Overcome in us the temptation to adopt the ways of the world for the work of Your kingdom in order to enjoy some success. You justify us by Your grace; now sanctify us also according to Your great mercy. In Christ, our Lord. Amen. (11)

> We speak as we are spoken to.
> God opens up our mouths, and
> out comes the Word He gives us
> to speak. The vocabulary of
> prayer is formed by the Word
> of God Himself.
> – Harold L. Senkbeil[36]

Thanksgiving upon Completion of Work

Almighty, eternal, and gracious God, I give You hearty thanks and praise for Your most holy aid and assistance shown me this day. Without You I surely could have done nothing, and therefore all praise belongs to You. I pray, be pleased with my work, and have it tend to the welfare, in body and soul, of myself and my fellow man; through Jesus Christ, our Lord. Amen. (12)

For Those Who Seek Employment

Father in heaven, giver of all good things, I thank You that You have created me and preserved me to this very day. I thank You for soundness of mind and body and for all schooling and training in preparation for a vocation. You know my needs and my fears because of my present unemployment. Comfort and help me to maintain my hope and courage.

It is clear from Your Word that work is normal and good for me, yet I have not yet found the work which I need and seek. This situation is hard to understand. Help me, Lord to surrender wholly to You and patiently seek Your Fatherly care and provision for my life.

As I wait, Lord, I pray that You would correct what is wrong with me or with my employment situation in general, and give me the opportunity to earn my bread. Open a door to employment that I do not now see. Keep me from being discouraged and bitter, and help me to put my trust in You for my employment too. Help me to say with a believing heart: "The eyes of all look to You, O Lord, and You give them their food at the proper time. You open Your hand and satisfy the desire of every living thing."

In that knowledge and in that faith make me trusting and patient. In the meantime care for me and mine according to Your promise. I trust You will do this for the sake of Jesus Christ, my Savior, in whom You have promised to give me all things. Amen. (13)

Prayer of Comfort Concerning Vocation

Dear Lord, I have Your Word and I am in the path of life that pleases You, this I know. Yet I look around and see how everywhere there is a lack of answers, a lack of help, and a lack of that which I need now! I can turn to no one for help except to You. Help me with all of this. My comfort is in this: You have said and commanded that I should ask, search and knock, and so doing I will certainly receive, find, and have that which I desire. Amen. (14)

For Joy in My Job

Heavenly Father, creator of heaven and earth, it is out of Your love and wisdom that You gave me work to do, and fitted me in body and mind to do this work. And yet my sinful will too often dreads the workday and casts about for other things to do. But You, O God, have called me to this work. Forgive me my sin. Strengthen me by Your Spirit that I may see that my place of work is a field of Your service to my family, my fellow worker, and to my neighbor. Give me joy in my vocation and make me glad and grateful for the strength to serve You; through Jesus Christ. Amen. (15)

When we learn to pray as Jesus taught, we learn that all prayer is corporate prayer, whether in church or by ourselves. We always pray in fellowship with the church even when we pray alone.

– Harold L. Senkbeil[35]

For My Family While I am Away

Gracious and good Lord, many perplexing thoughts run through my mind to disturb and irritate me. I know You are acquainted with all my thinking. I and mine are precious to You. I know therefore that You will watch over each member of my family and keep us, one and all, in Your grace. That You have promised to do. Grant that I will not grow cold and indifferent toward You because I am not hedged in and protected by my family at home. Give me the grace to continue in Your worship and come to Your altar to receive Your body and blood in Your Holy Communion as do those I have left behind at home. There we meet, Lord God, even when we are miles apart, and join the whole company of heaven in praise even while we receive the comfort of Your forgiveness for our sins.

Keep our faith strong and our lives unsullied by sin. Give me and each one of the family the grace to accept with cheerfulness and courage whatever befalls us. Let Your Word be our light and our peace at all times. Above all, let the day be not too far off when we can be united in our home and together in worship and praise of You as our heavenly Father in Christ Jesus who has promised to be with us always, no matter where we are. Hear my prayer for Jesus' sake. Amen. (16)

At the Beginning Or End of a School Year

Lord, God, You have called Your servants to ventures of which we cannot see the ending, by paths as yet untrodden, through perils unknown. Give us faith to go out with good courage, not knowing where we go but only that Your hand is leading us and Your love supporting us; through Jesus Christ, Our Lord. (17)

For Life Together at This College/University

Almighty and most merciful God, we pray Your blessing on all who are joined together at this (college/university): students, faculty, and staff. Grant that we may so work and study, think and pray, grow and relax together, that we may be more perfectly fitted to serve You and our brothers and sisters in the work You have given and will give us to do. Help us to look wide, fill us with high ideals, give us love and good will to all people; and above all, keep us faithful to You under the Cross of our Savior, Jesus Christ, who died and rose for us, that we might always be Yours. (18)

For Proper Study

Heavenly Father, let Your favor rest on my studies this day. Discipline my mind in the search for truth, and enable me to grasp it; but grant that as I increase in the knowledge of Your world, I may grow to know You better through your Incarnate Word, for to know You is life eternal. I pray in the name of Jesus Christ, Your Son and my Savior. (19)

Before Examinations

Lord God, as I face this examination free me from all anxiety and grant me a quiet mind, clear memory, and accurate comprehension of what I have studied, and keep me honest in thought and action; for the sake of my Lord Jesus Christ. (20)

Being Single

Merciful Father, You have promised to sustain us, Your children, throughout our earthly pilgrimage, whatever it may be that You have planned. St. Paul, as a single person, lived out his entire earthly pilgrimage willingly with graciousness and thanksgiving. I fervently pray that You will sustain me with the same spirit. Grant me the willingness to accept my vocation as a single person and grant me sustenance through the Body of Christ.

Continue to surround me with family and friends and grant me the opportunity to serve You and Your church. Finally, grant me the ability to live out my earthly pilgrimage with contentment and joy. Amen. (21)

Before Travel

Lord God our Father, You kept Abraham and Sarah in safety throughout the days of their pilgrimage, You led the children of Israel through the midst of the sea, and by a star You led the Wise Men to the infant Jesus. Protect and guide me now in this time as I set out to travel, make my ways safe and my homecoming joyful, and bring me at last to my heavenly home; through Jesus Christ, Your Son, our Lord. Amen. (22)

The brother of the Law is compulsion, the sister of freedom is gladness. When the Holy Spirit is the teacher He leads on to a cheerful spirit. The one who walks in the "flesh" brings a grudging sacrifice, but he who is led by the Spirit finds gladness in sacrifice and surrender.
– Albert Koberle[37]

Prayer of Blessing
for an Apartment / Dorm / House

O Lord, as I enter into my new home/apartment/dorm, come with me and let Your divine presence bless me with the riches of Your grace. Guard my entering and leaving. Grant that I may keep out of this home all selfishness, pride, and thoughtlessness. Let Your Word abide among all who enter here, that knowing first Your love-bought peace, I may love and be at peace with my/our neighbors, and that by our living I may bring glory and honor to You as the Master of this household and the defender of this home; through Jesus Christ our Lord. (23)

Looking for a Godly Spouse

O You almighty, eternal God, Creator, Preserver and Multiplier of the human race, You instituted marriage while Adam and Eve still dwelt in paradise. You also honored holy matrimony by the first miracle performed by Your dear Son, Jesus Christ, our Savior, at the wedding in Cana of Galilee. You know my heart; You know my disposition and attributes, and You know weaknesses and strengths better than I myself. From You one also receives the gift of a good spouse because that comes alone from the Most High. I beseech You from the heart that You would grant me a good,

Christian, God-fearing spouse whom I would ever hold dear in my heart. I pray that this companion and I might peacefully and harmoniously live upon earth in the true fear of God and in this Christian journey. I cry to You, make my heart fit regarding such things, and enlighten me with Your Holy Spirit. And having commended the matter to Your fatherly care, let me be at peace; for the sake of Jesus Christ. Amen. (24)

When I Am Disappointed by Love

Lord Jesus, You are the lover of my soul and will never leave me nor forsake me. Your tender mercy is from everlasting, and Your truth endures to all generations.

You have known the frailty and fickleness of men. You know how often I myself have betrayed Your love and trifled with Your goodness. Forgive me, Lord Jesus, for being lukewarm to Your love, cool to the offers of Your grace, and forgetful of Your sacrifice upon the cross.

Help me to be kind, tenderhearted, and forgiving, even as God, my Father, for Your sake has forgiven me. Remove all bitterness from my heart, and enable me to show true love to the one who has hurt me.

In the midst of my disappointment, give me the grace to be honest with myself and with You, lest I become proud and refuse to recognize my own shortcomings. If I have driven human love away by being loveless or unlovable, teach me to return to You for pardon and for the warmth of Your enduring love.

When it pleases You, give me the love of one who will pattern his (her) love after Yours and then give me the grace to do the same. In Jesus' name I ask it. Amen. (25)

Strife in the Home

Father of all who blesses us beyond measure, You placed us together that we might be a help to each other, that we would support and strengthen the other not only for the trials of this life, but also in faith and for the life to come. Have mercy on us; for I have not lived my life according to Your will and by choosing my will over Yours, I have brought strife into my home.

O God, You know how prone my heart is to mistrust, temper, lack of patience and strife. Forgive me for praying so little, for my want of love, for stubbornly insisting on my rights and my own way. Come to us and help us. Make us to know again that without Your peace our hearts will have no peace. Give us, O God, the will and the means to be reconciled to You and to one another; join us to Yourself through Word and Sacrament that we may live together and with You in the peace that only You can give; through Your Son, our Lord Jesus Christ. Amen. (26)

In Times of Doubt

Lord, I am troubled by many things, and in my trouble I am inclined to forget You and in my own weakness I sometimes doubt Your ability or desire to help. In health and prosperity I am inclined to forget You and ascribe my successes to myself and to my hard and intelligent work. I know that all this is the empty boasting of my sinful pride, and my forgetfulness of You. I must humble myself and in the dust of my sinfulness say: "Lord I believe; help my unbelief."

Gracious Father, help me always to remember that You are God; that You have given me my body and soul, my food and clothing, home and family, and all that I have; that You defend me from all harm and danger and guard and protect me from all evil and the assaults of the Devil; not because of any merit or worthiness of my own, but only out of Your fatherly goodness and mercy.

Help me always to remember, Lord Jesus, that You are true God and true Man; that You shed Your holy precious blood for me to redeem me from my sin, from eternal death, that I might be Yours forever.

Help me always to remember, Lord God, Holy Spirit, that You have called me by the Gospel and brought me to faith in my Lord and Savior Jesus Christ, that I have forgiveness of sins and eternal salvation through such faith, and that You have promised to keep me in the saving faith until my dying day.

Yes, Lord, help me to remember what You have graciously done for me, and in that remembrance help me to trust in You for all my needs, for I am Your beloved child. In that knowledge help me to live joyfully and confidently, and to die gloriously; through Jesus Christ. Amen. (27)

In Times of Loneliness

O Lord, my God, you have said: "I will never leave you nor forsake you." Yet I feel forsaken and alone. You have assured me that nothing can separate me from Your love in Christ Jesus, my Lord. And yet my heart is distressed by a deadening sense of loneliness.

Lord, to whom shall I go? I believe and am sure that You have the words of eternal life. Strengthen me in my faith, and grant me a fuller measure of comfort from Your sure presence.

Lord, give me the grace in my loneliness to search my soul as to its cause. If I am lonely because I have refused to give myself in service to others, forgive me for contributing to my loneliness by my own selfishness. If I am lonely because of loyalty to You and Your Gospel, help me to rejoice in my cross-bearing.

Preserve me from all temptation to forget Your watchful presence when I am alone, lest I fall into sin and shame. Direct my thoughts heavenward, bring me into the fellowship of other believers, and use me as a means of bringing joy and blessings to others. Teach me to pray: "Why are you cast down, O my soul, and why are you disturbed within me? Hope in God; for I shall yet praise Him who is the health of my countenance and my God." Amen. (28)

In Times of Temptation

Almighty God and merciful Father, from before time You have known me and in the womb You so wonderfully fashioned me. You know too the inmost thoughts, my thoughts and desires. I am set in the midst of many and great temptations that threaten to capture the frailty of my flesh and my natural inclination for the things of this world. Lord, have mercy on me! Strengthen me by Your grace that I may always stand upright; grant me the strength and protection against all dangers; and carry me through the temptations of this world; through Jesus Christ, Your Son, our Lord. Amen. (29)

During Personal Illness

Divine Lord, You have been gracious and merciful to me in Christ Jesus. Forgive me all my sins day after day. Accept my thanks for this Your goodness. Let me find my joy in You who has brought to my heart salvation and peace.

In Your mercy look upon my distress and pain, and forgive me all my sins and all my worry. Ease my sufferings, and make me patient and cheerful in my affliction. Bless those who take care of me. Let them not become weary in this service that they must render to me. Keep me faithful to Your Word, and grant that I may continue in Your grace until life's journey ends and I behold You in the glory of eternity, through Jesus Christ, our Lord. Amen. (30)

Passing the Course

Revelation 3:1–11

"Behold, I come quickly;
hold that fast which thou hast,
that no man take thy crown."

As the professor walked into the classroom, he announced that he would now give the class a quick quiz. For some students this quiz was easy. They had daily kept up with their assignments and studied their notes, so they knew all the answers. For others, however, this test was a surprise. The students who were prepared got an A, those who were unprepared got a D or F.

This story may sound familiar to many of us, but the idea behind the story can be applied to all of us in our everyday lives as Christian students. There will be a day when we will all be called into the classroom of judgment by the Lord Himself, who is greater than any professor or dean. At that time we will need more than knowledge; we will need faith in Jesus Christ as our Savior. If we have sincere faith in Jesus Christ, the result will be much more valuable than an A; it will be eternal salvation in God's holy kingdom. But without true faith, which works by love, the result will be much worse than an F; it will be eternal separation from God.

As the passage above indicates, God comes quickly. Therefore one cannot prepare for the judgment test by cramming the night before the exam or quickly skimming notes, but rather by diligently studying the textbook of God's holy Word, believing that God's Son died for our sins, and by living in the true Christian spirit of love.

Of course, there are always temptations for us to be drawn away from God's Word just as there are temptations to cut classes. God offers us faith strong enough to overcome these temptations and to hold fast to His Word with the help of the Holy Spirit. These temptations from the devil come to us in a variety of ways, and we must recognize them so we can combat them with our faith and knowledge in God. Envying a classmate's good grades or expensive clothes, cutting Bible class to go to a movie, not going to church because of a roommate's sarcastic remarks about your religion— these are the "quick quizzes" that test your faith. What kind of grade would you receive on these tests of temptation? Would you fail and continue to drift further from God's Word, or would you pass and receive the crown of eternal life and salvation? As St. Paul reminds us: "Now is our salvation nearer than when we first believed*." [38]

* Romans 13:11

When in the hour of deepest need
We know not where to look for aid;
When days and nights of anxious thought
No help or counsel yet have brought,

Our comfort then is this alone,
That we may meet before your throne
And cry to you, O faithful God,
For rescue from our sorry lot.

For you have made a promise true
To pardon those who flee to you,
Through him whose name alone is great,
Our Savior and our advocate.

And so we come, O God, today
And all our woes before you lay;
For sorely tried, cast down, we stand,
Perplexed by fears on ev'ry hand.

Oh, from our sins hide not your face;
Absolve us through your boundless grace!
Be with us in our anguish still!
Free us at last from ev'ry ill!

So we with all our hearts each day
To you our glad thanksgiving pay,
Then walk obedient to your Word,
And now and ever praise you, Lord. (*LW* 428)

Text: Paul Eber

The Teaching and Practice
of Private Confession

My dear Christian, when you go to confession, do not be content with repeating a memorized confessional prayer or with having your pastor repeat it to you. Rather, bring along a penitent heart, from which your confession will flow. To offer confession when the heart is impenitent is mocking God. Without a penitent heart there is no forgiveness of sin.

The first requirement for a penitent heart is that you recognize your sins, feel sorry and repentant of them. By nature no man knows his sins, nor can he by his own doing cause repentance to spring from his heart. On the contrary, repentance comes from God. By nature we are far too blind, too indifferent, too careless, too self-righteous, too much absorbed in self-love and self-conceit, to plead guilty of all sins in the sight of God.

Above all things therefore bow your knees before God and call upon Him to open your eyes that you may thoroughly recognize the multitude and magnitude of your sins. Pray in the words of the sainted David: "Search me, O God, and know my heart! Try me and know my thoughts! And see if there be any grievous way in me, and lead me in the way everlasting" (Psalm 139:23–24). Make a careful examination of your whole life according to the Ten Commandments. You will then soon find that you are a sinner. For even as a man does not see a spot on his face without a mirror, so he does not recognize his sins unless he sees himself in the mirror of the holy Ten Commandments. For every thought, every word, every deed against God's commandments is a sin, whether it consists in doing what God has forbidden or in failing to do what He has commanded.

> We believe in Christ. Christ dwells within us and "he who is in you is greater than he who is in the world." The victory does not depend on our faith, but on Christ, to whom faith holds fast. And therefore a struggling faith, which feels itself weak can be so much stronger than a faith which feels itself strong because it relies on its experiences, its warmth, and its earlier victories. If God permits us to fail, then it may be that he wishes us to learn to rely entirely on Christ.
> — Bo Giertz[40]

But you must look not only at the large, external sins, but also those internal, secret digressions from God's commandments, the evil thoughts and desires of your heart. When examining yourself, being instant in prayer, you will discover that you did not fear, love, and trust in God as He demands; that you have not called upon God in prayer, praise, and thanksgiving so heartily and confidently as you should have done; that you have not properly heard and learned His Word and kept it sacred. You will find that you have not duly honored and obeyed your parents and superiors, but that you have been disobedient and discourteous toward them; that you have sinned against your neighbor by being angry, revengeful, and unforgiving; by entertaining unholy thoughts and desires; by showing envy, covetousness, and a sinful mind or by speaking slanderous words.

This is how we deal with guilt: the bitterness of sins confessed and the sweet truth of sins absolved and gone forever in Jesus, name. He places his forgiveness into the preaching of the gospel, into Holy Baptism, into the Lord's Supper, and into holy absolution. He takes our guilt and gives us forgiveness, life, and salvation. And by grace, through faith, we receive the peace of mind and heart that is the joy and peace of Christ himself!"

–Harold L. Senkbeil[42]

To sum up, you will come to know that you did not love your neighbor uprightly and heartily as yourself; rather, that self-love, quest for personal gain and honor, was the moving force of all your actions. Because of these and other sins you indeed have deserved God's wrath, temporal and eternal punishment, if God would deal with you strictly according to justice. From these sins that you notice in yourself you can infer how unclean and polluted your heart must be from which these sins flow; for the stream is no purer than its fountain, and by its fruits the tree is known. In this way you will come to a true knowledge of original sin.

Consider also the sins you do not know, but still have committed. They are far more numerous than those you do know. The omniscient God places all your sins in the light of His countenance. Knowing this, you certainly will be terrified in your conscience and experience sorrow and contrition for having offended your loving God so grievously and for having repaid His mercies with such dishonorable ingratitude.

The second part of repentance is faith, faith in Jesus Christ. It is He who has rendered full satisfaction for all your sins, procuring forgiveness of them all. Faith is, so to speak, the hand that appropriates forgiveness of sin and accepts it as an unmerited gift of divine grace. Without this faith all knowledge of sin and penitence over it is nothing but the repentance of a Cain and of a Judas and must end in despair. But by faith in Jesus Christ, the Savior of all sinners, the heart is comforted and satisfied. This faith, however, you cannot bring forth yourself; it is the work and gift of God the Holy Spirit. But if you feel that your faith is weak—you desire to believe, but you think you cannot—then pray to God to strengthen this faith of yours, which is battling against doubt. He is willing to do so and surely will give you a stronger faith, so that you will overcome all the doubts which are troubling your soul.

If you come to confession with such a penitent and believing heart, you will rejoice in the absolution spoken by your pastor. For your sins are really and truly forgiven by God in heaven. Such forgiveness of sins Christ has procured for all sinners by the shedding of His blood and by His death, and by His resurrection He sealed it to them. This He commanded to preach throughout the world by means of the Gospel. Therefore when your pastor absolves you, he does nothing else than proclaim to you the Gospel of the forgiveness of sins. This, however, is not an empty announcement, but one actually offering and conveying the forgiveness of sins to the penitent sinner. Whenever, therefore, you hear your pastor pronounce absolution, do not doubt, but firmly believe, that your sins are forgiven before God in heaven. Believe it as firmly as though Christ were calling to you directly from heaven: "Take heart, My son [my daughter]; your sins are forgiven" (Matthew 9:2). For He says: "The One who hears you hears Me" (Luke 10:16); and: "If you forgive the sins of anyone, they are forgiven" (John 20:23).

Then the fruits of repentance are to follow. These consist in no longer knowingly and intentionally committing such sins as were forgiven you, but rather hating them, abstaining from them, and battling against them with the assistance of the Holy Spirit.

> The modern world came into being in the course of the struggle against ecclesiastical dogma which took place around the turn of the eighteenth century. Since that time, resentment against everything which confession, doctrine, and the dogma of the church mean exists at the very heart of modern man, even the modern man of the church and in his theology. Just when one boasts of a rediscovery of the church's confession, one often finds a subconscious flight from dogma, a flight from the doctrinal content of that confession."
> —Hermann Sasse[41]

A Prayer of One Preparing for Confession and Absolution

Lord Jesus Christ, Son of God, have mercy on me, a sinner! Your Word is a lamp unto my feet and a light upon my path. It has laid bare my sin, for which I deserve nothing but punishment; yet, it has also declared to me Your grace and mercy and forgiveness.

As You have taught my heart to believe and trust in You, so shall I also confess with my mouth. Grant me the honesty to examine my life according to Your holy Ten Commandments, especially as they address my vocations in life. Discipline me as Your beloved child. Enable me to recognize my sin, to know and feel it in my heart, and rightly to bemoan and lament my iniquity and offenses. Give me both humility and courage to confess my sins to receive from him Your Holy Absolution, according to Your good and gracious will. Invigorate my faith, through this same word of forgiveness, to have no doubt, but firmly to believe, that by it all my sins are forgiven before God in heaven.

You have called and sent my pastor, in Your name and stead, to hear my confession with Your ears of mercy, and to forgive me with Your own voice. Since You have chosen to deal with me in this way, allow me not to neglect Your gift but to lay hold of it with eager confidence. Create in me a clean heart, O God, and restore to me the joy of Your salvation; for Your Name's sake. Amen.

FIRST COMMANDMENT

You shall have no other gods.

What or whom do I fear most?

In what or whom do I trust most for financial security, physical safety, or emotional support?

Do I fear God's wrath and therefore avoid every sin?

Do I expect only good from God in every situation, or do I worry, doubt, complain, or feel unfairly treated when things go wrong?

SECOND COMMANDMENT

You shall not misuse the name of the Lord your God.

Does the Gospel adorn my daily speech and conduct, or do I curse, speak carelessly, or misuse God's name?

Have I kept all the vows I have made in the Lord's Name?

Am I diligent and sincere in my prayers, or have I been lazy, bored or distracted? Do I trust that the Lord God will answer them according to His good and gracious will?

THIRD COMMANDMENT

Remember the Sabbath Day by keeping it holy.

Do I despise the Word by neglect or by paying little or no attention when it is read or preached?

Am I faithful in the Divine Service, or do I attend sporadically, preferring to be elsewhere when the Church is at worship?

Do I pray for my pastor and support his efforts to guard Christ's flock from error?

FOURTH COMMANDMENT

Honor your father and your mother.

Do I submit to those whom God has put in authority over me?

Have I been ashamed of, angry, stubborn, or disrespectful toward my parents, teachers, employer, pastor, government or other authorities?

Do I obey all the laws of the city, state and country, and pay my rightful share of all taxes?

FIFTH COMMANDMENT

You shall not murder.

Do I hate anyone, or am I angry with anyone?
Do I hold grudges or harbor resentment?

Am I abusive (in word or deed) toward my spouse, children, or anyone else?

Have I ignored the plight of the helpless or been callous toward genuine need?

You shall not commit adultery.

Have I held in highest regard God's gift of sexuality or have I debased it in any way by my thoughts, words or conduct?

Am I guilty of lust, indecency, or the use of pornography (either in print or on the Internet)?

Have I reserved my sexual activity for the pleasure and consolation of my spouse, and when God wills, the procreation of children?

You shall not steal.

Have I gotten anything in a dishonest way?

Have I made illegal copies of any printed material, audio or video tapes, or computer programs?

Do I take care of what I have, pay what I owe, return what I borrow, and respect other people's property?

Do I avoid excessive debt?

Do I give generously, or am I selfish, stingy and greedy with my time and money?

You shall not give false testimony against your neighbor.

Do I speak the truth or have I lied in any way?

Do I gossip or take pleasure in talking about the faults and mistakes of others?

Have I judged others without being duly authorized?

Have I gladly and willingly found ways to explain in the best possible way the words or actions of those who hurt me?

Am I the first to admit my own mistakes, or do I cover up my sins and make myself look better than I am?

You shall not covet your neighbor's house.

Do I have strong wants, desires, or cravings that consume my thoughts?

Do I resent those who have more than I?

Do I neglect my marriage, family, church and other relationships in a desperate attempt to secure more?

Have my wants kept me from being happy with and thankful for what God has given me?

*You shall not covet your neighbor's wife,
or his manservant or maidservant, his ox or
donkey, or anything that belongs to your neighbor.*

Am I discontent with the spouse the Lord God
has given me?

Am I discontent with the job I have or the
employees I supervise?

Have I neglected to urge someone to remain
faithful to his or her spouse?

Have I wanted my neighbor's husband or wife,
boyfriend or girlfriend, workers or property to be
mine?

> The Holy Spirit
> does not intoxicate
> and stupefy but
> produces a holy sobriety.
> —Albert Koberle[43]

An Act of Confession
A Brief Order for Confession and Absolution

Based on Luther's Small Catechism

You may prepare yourself by meditation on the Ten Commandments and by praying Psalms 6, 7, 13, 15, 51, 121, or 130.

When you are ready, you may kneel and say:

Dear pastor, I ask you to hear my confession and pronounce my forgiveness according to God's will.

Proceed.

I, a poor sinner, plead guilty before God of all my sins.

I have lived as if God did not matter and as if I mattered most. My Lord's name I have not honored as I should; my worship and prayers have faltered.

I have not let His love have its way with me, and so my love for others has failed.

There are those whom I have hurt, and those whom I failed to help.

My thoughts and desires have been soiled with sin.

If you wish to confess specific sins that trouble you, continue as follows:

What troubles me particularly is that . . .

Confess whatever you have done against the commandments of God and your own place in life.

Then conclude by saying:

Have mercy on me, O God, according to your steadfast love; according to your abundant mercy blot out my transgressions.

Wash me thoroughly from my iniquity, and cleanse me from my sin! For I know my transgressions, and my sin is ever before me. (Psalm 51:1–3)

God be merciful to you and strengthen your faith.

Amen.

Do you believe that my forgiveness is God's forgiveness?

Yes.

Let it be done for you as you believe. In the stead and by the command of my Lord Jesus Christ, I forgive you all your sins: In the name of the Father and of the ✝ Son and of the Holy Spirit.

Amen.

Go in peace.

Amen.

Why Am I in College Anyway?

Everyone on campus has reasons for being in college. What are yours? If asked, each student could come up with some kind of answer. What would yours be? A campus pastor once discussed attending the university with a large group of young people who were nearing the age to enter. Practically all wanted to attend the university. All gave reasons. But it was apparent that many of those present had not given much thorough consideration to the subject. This is true of some who have been in college for some time. When was the last time you gave serious thought to the question "Why am I in college anyway?"

The discussion mentioned above provided a variety of reasons for a college career—"get better jobs," "find a mate," "have a ball," "it's the thing to do these days," even "not have to work for a while." Only after these and other motivations were mentioned did someone say what you could claim was obvious for the Christian student: "to develop my God-given talents for better service to my Lord Jesus and my fellow man." No one would say that those who have no opportunity to attend college have fewer talents than those who do. But those with such an opportunity have a good chance to develop that ability and learn skills.

In our days when material advantage is so emphasized, when values are shifting and Christian values often overshadowed, the words of the ancient and very wise writer of Proverbs are particularly straight to the point of this meditation:

> "Blessed is the one who finds wisdom, and the one who gets understanding, for the gain from her is better than gain from silver and her profit better than gold." (3:13–14)

Jesus emphasized this understanding and the maturity that comes with the Lord's wisdom when He said, "Seek first the kingdom of God and His righteousness, and all these things will be added to you" (Matthew 6:33). As a Christian student you can seek the kingdom and righteousness of God in all your efforts because He has first sought and found you. You belong to Him. His Holy Spirit has called you by the Gospel, enlightened you with His gifts, sanctified and kept you in the true faith. Assured of the forgiveness of sins and new life in Jesus Christ, your student days can be beautiful days of discipleship. This life of discipleship includes the wisdom of knowing why you are in college and in whose service you are engaged.[44]

The man is ever blessed
Who shuns the sinners' ways,
Among their counsels never stands,
Nor takes the scorners' place.

But makes the Law of God
His study and delight
Amid the labors of the day
And watches of the night.

He like a tree shall thrive,
With waters near the root;
Fresh as the leaf his name shall live,
His works are heav'nly fruit.

Not so the wicked race,
They no such blessings find;
Their hopes shall flee like empty chaff
Before the driving wind.

How will they bear to stand
Before the judgment seat
Where all the saints at Christ's right hand
In full assembly meet?

He knows and he approves
The way the righteous go;
But sinners and their works shall meet
A dreadful overthrow. (*LW* 388)

Text: Isaac Watts

A Brief Summary
of the Christian Faith

This is the text of Dr. Martin Luther's Small Catechism, the most popular explanation of the central teachings of the Christian faith. It has been used by countless Christians of all denominations for almost 500 years.

—THE TEN COMMANDMENTS—

As the head of the family should teach them in a simple way to his household

The First Commandment—

You shall have no other gods.

What does this mean? We should fear, love, and trust in God above all things.

The Second Commandment—

You shall not misuse the name of the Lord your God.

What does this mean? We should fear and love God so that we do not curse, swear, use satanic arts, lie, or deceive by His name, but call upon it in every trouble, pray, praise, and give thanks.

The Third Commandment—

Remember the Sabbath day by keeping it holy.

What does this mean? We should fear and love God so that we do not despise preaching and His Word, but hold it sacred and gladly hear and learn it.

The Fourth Commandment—

Honor your father and your mother.

What does this mean? We should fear and love God so that we do not despise or anger our parents and other authorities, but honor them, serve and obey them, love and cherish them.

The Fifth Commandment—

You shall not murder.

What does this mean? We should fear and love God so that we do not hurt or harm our neighbor in his body, but help and support him in every physical need.

> Freedom in Christ and the love that it inspires do not in this life reap the rewards that they deserve. But since the love of God remains the constant, Christians will go on believing and will go on loving, no matter what."
>
> —Henry Hamann[45]

The Sixth Commandment—

You shall not commit adultery.

What does this mean? We should fear and love God so that we lead a sexually pure and decent life in what we say and do, and husband and wife love and honor each other.

The Seventh Commandment—

You shall not steal.

What does this mean? We should fear and love God so that we do not take our neighbor's money or possessions, or get them in any dishonest way, but help him to improve and protect his possessions and income.

The Eighth Commandment—

You shall not give false testimony against your neighbor.

What does this mean? We should fear and love God so that we do not tell lies about our neighbor, betray him, slander him, or hurt his reputation, but defend him, speak well of him, and explain everything in the kindest way.

The more truly we hold fast to the 'God-for-us,' the more 'our-being-for-God' grows and is strengthened.
—Albert Koberle [49]

The Ninth Commandment—

You shall not covet your neighbor's house.

What does this mean? We should fear and love God so that we do not scheme to get our neighbor's inheritance or house, or get it in a way which only appears right, but help and be of service to him in keeping it.

The Tenth Commandment—

You shall not covet your neighbor's wife, or his manservant or maidservant, his ox or donkey, or anything that belongs to your neighbor.

What does this mean? We should fear and love God so that we do not entice or force away our neighbor's wife, workers, or animals, or turn them against him, but urge them to stay and do their duty.

[The text of the commandments is from Exodus 20:3, 7–8, 12–17.]

The Close of the Commandments—

What does God say about all these commandments? He says: "I, the Lord your God, am a jealous God, punishing the children for the sin of the fathers to the third and fourth generation of those who hate Me, but showing love to a thousand generations of those who love Me and keep My commandments." [Exodus 20:5–6]

What does this mean? God threatens to punish all who break these commandments. Therefore, we should fear His wrath and not do anything against them. But He promises grace and every blessing to all who keep these commandments. Therefore, we should also love and trust in Him and gladly do what He commands.

> The Christian Faith does not have to do with myth because it does not believe in gods, but in the One Almighty God. To be sure, it has something which corresponds to the myth of natural religion. . . . The victory march of the ancient church meant, among other things, that Christian dogma took the place of fading myths, just as happens in reverse today. Where Christian dogma wanes or decays, myth returns in modern form.
> —Hermann Sasse[48]

As the head of the family should teach it in a simple way to his household

The First Article—

I believe in God, the Father Almighty, Maker of heaven and earth.

What does this mean? I believe that God has made me and all creatures; that He has given me my body and soul, eyes, ears, and all my members, my reason and all my senses, and still takes care of them.

He also gives me clothing and shoes, food and drink, house and home, wife and children, land, animals, and all I have. He richly and daily provides me with all that I need to support this body and life.

He defends me against all danger and guards and protects me from all evil.

All this He does only out of fatherly, divine goodness and mercy, without any merit or worthiness in me. For all this it is my duty to thank and praise, to serve and obey Him.

This is most certainly true.

The Second Article—

And in Jesus Christ, His only Son, our Lord, who was conceived by the Holy Spirit, born of the Virgin Mary, suffered under Pontius Pilate, was crucified, died and was buried. He descended into hell. The third day He rose again from the dead. He ascended into heaven and sits at the right hand of God the Father Almighty. From thence He will come to judge the living and the dead.

What does this mean? I believe that Jesus Christ, true God, begotten of the Father from eternity, and also true man, born of the Virgin Mary, is my Lord, who has redeemed me, a lost and condemned person, purchased and won me from all sins, from death, and from the power of the devil; not with gold or silver, but with His holy, precious blood and with His innocent suffering and death, that I may be His own and live under Him in His kingdom, and serve Him in everlasting righteousness, innocence, and blessedness, just as He is risen from the dead, lives and reigns to all eternity.

This is most certainly true.

The Third Article—

I believe in the Holy Spirit, the holy Christian Church, the communion of saints, the forgiveness of sins, the resurrection of the body, and the life everlasting. Amen

What does this mean? I believe that I cannot by my own reason or strength believe in Jesus Christ, my Lord, or come to Him; but the Holy Spirit has called me by the Gospel, enlightened me with His gifts, sanctified and kept me in the true faith.

In the same way He calls, gathers, enlightens, and sanctifies the whole Christian Church on earth and keeps it with Jesus Christ in the one true faith.

In this Christian Church He daily and richly forgives all my sins and the sins of all believers.

On the Last Day He will raise me and all the dead, and give eternal life to me and all believers in Christ.

This is most certainly true.

> When we exhort people to Faith as a virtue, to the settled intention of continuing to believe certain things, we are not exhorting them to fight against reason. The intention of continuing to believe is required because, though Reason is divine, human reasoners are not.
> —C. S. Lewis[47]

As the head of the family should teach it in a simple way to his household

Our Father, who art in heaven, hallowed be Thy name, Thy kingdom come, Thy will be done on earth as it is in heaven. Give us this day our daily bread; and forgive us our trespasses as we forgive those who trespass against us; and lead us not into temptation, but deliver us from evil. For Thine is the kingdom and the power and the glory forever and ever. Amen.

The Introduction—

Our Father who art in heaven.

What does this mean? With these words God tenderly invites us to believe that He is our true Father and that we are His true children, so that with all boldness and confidence we may ask Him as dear children ask their dear father.

The First Petition—

Hallowed be Thy name.

What does this mean? God's name is certainly holy in itself, but we pray in this petition that it may be kept holy among us also.

How is God's name kept holy? God's name is kept holy when the Word of God is taught in its truth and purity, and we, as the children of God, also lead holy lives according to it. Help us to do this, dear Father in heaven! But anyone who teaches or lives contrary to God's Word profanes the name of God among us. Protect us from this, heavenly Father!

The Second Petition—

Thy kingdom come.

What does this mean? The kingdom of God certainly comes by itself without our prayer, but we pray in this petition that it may come to us also.

How does God's kingdom come? God's kingdom comes when our heavenly Father gives us His Holy Spirit, so that by His grace we believe His holy Word and lead godly lives here in time and there in eternity.

The Third Petition—

Thy will be done on earth as it is in heaven.

What does this mean? The good and gracious will of God is done even without our prayer, but we pray in this petition that it may be done among us also.

How is God's will done? God's will is done when He breaks and hinders every evil plan and purpose of the devil, the world, and our sinful nature, which do not want us to hallow God's name or let His kingdom come; and when He strengthens and keeps us firm in His Word and faith until we die.

This is His good and gracious will.

The Fourth Petition—

Give us this day our daily bread.

What does this mean? God certainly gives daily bread to everyone without our prayers, even to all evil people, but we pray in this petition that God would lead us to realize this and to receive our daily bread with thanksgiving.

What is meant by daily bread? Daily bread includes everything that has to do with the support and needs of the body, such as food, drink, clothing, shoes, house, home, land, animals, money, goods, a devout husband or wife, devout children, devout workers, devout and faithful rulers, good government, good weather, peace, health, self-control, good reputation, good friends, faithful neighbors, and the like.

The Fifth Petition—

And forgive us our trespasses as we forgive those who trespass against us.

What does this mean? We pray in this petition that our Father in heaven would not look at our sins, or deny our prayer because of them. We are neither worthy of the things for which we pray, nor have we deserved them, but we ask that He would give them all to us by grace, for we daily sin much and surely deserve nothing but punishment. So we too will sincerely forgive and gladly do good to those who sin against us.

> The work of the Holy Spirit leads us to the assurance of faith. . . . We cannot always feel such assurance. But even when we are perplexed and disturbed within, the Spirit may be at work in our hearts. The sign that he has not forsaken us is the fact that we not forsaken the Word and that Word constantly awakens repentance and faith.
>
> – Bo Giertz[45]

The Sixth Petition—

And lead us not into temptation.

What does this mean? God tempts no one. We pray in this petition that God would guard and keep us so that the devil, the world, and our sinful nature may not deceive us or mislead us into false belief, despair, and other great shame and vice. Although we are attacked by these things, we pray that we may finally overcome them and win the victory.

The Seventh Petition—

But deliver us from evil.

What does this mean? We pray in this petition, in summary, that our Father in heaven would rescue us from every evil of body and soul, possessions and reputation, and finally, when our last hour comes, give us a blessed end, and graciously take us from this valley of sorrow to Himself in heaven.

The Conclusion—

For Thine is the kingdom and the power and the glory forever and ever. Amen.

What does this mean? This means that I should be certain that these petitions are pleasing to our Father in heaven, and are heard by Him; for He Himself has commanded us to pray in this way and has promised to hear us. Amen, amen means "yes, yes, it shall be so."

As the head of the family should teach it in a simple way to his household

> We are all merely like infants at holy baptism. As believers we are merely those who say, "I believe, dear Lord, help my unbelief." We must recognize that unbelief, the human incapability to believe in God is the same for all the children of Adam, and that faith in every case is a psychologically inconceivable miracle of God.
>
> —Hermann Sasse [50]

First—

What is Baptism?

Baptism is not just plain water, but it is the water included in God's command and combined with God's word.

Which is that word of God?

Christ our Lord says in the last chapter of Matthew: **"Therefore go and make disciples of all nations, baptizing them in the name of the Father and of the Son and of the Holy Spirit."** *[Matthew 28:19]*

Second—

What benefits does Baptism give?

It works forgiveness of sins, rescues from death and the devil, and gives eternal salvation to all who believe this, as the words and promises of God declare.

Which are these words and promises of God?

Christ our Lord says in the last chapter of Mark: **"Whoever believes and is baptized will be saved, but whoever does not believe will be condemned."** *[Mark 16:16]*

Third—

How can water do such great things?

Certainly not just water, but the word of God in and with the water does these things, along with the faith which trusts this word of God in the water. For without God's word the water is plain water and no Baptism. But with the word of God it is a Baptism, that is, a life-giving water, rich in grace, and a washing of the new birth in the Holy Spirit, as St. Paul says in Titus chapter three:

"He saved us through the washing of rebirth and renewal by the Holy Spirit, whom He poured out on us generously through Jesus Christ our Savior, so that, having been justified by His grace, we might become heirs having the hope of eternal life. This is a trustworthy saying." *[Titus 3:5–8]*

Fourth—

What does such baptizing with water indicate?

It indicates that the Old Adam in us should by daily contrition and repentance be drowned and die with all sins and evil desires, and that a new man should daily emerge and arise to live before God in righteousness and purity forever.

Where is this written?

St. Paul writes in Romans chapter six: "We were therefore buried with Him through baptism into death in order that, just as Christ was raised from the dead through the glory of the Father, we too may live a new life." *[Romans 6:4]*

How Christians should be taught to confess

What is Confession?

Confession has two parts.

First, that we confess our sins, and second, that we receive absolution, that is, forgiveness, from the pastor as from God Himself, not doubting, but firmly believing that by it our sins are forgiven before God in heaven.

What sins should we confess?

Before God we should plead guilty of all sins, even those we are not aware of, as we do in the Lord's Prayer; but before the pastor we should confess only those sins which we know and feel in our hearts.

Which are these?

Consider your place in life according to the Ten Commandments: Are you a father, mother, son, daughter, husband, wife, or worker? Have you been disobedient, unfaithful, or lazy? Have you been hot-tempered, rude, or quarrelsome? Have you hurt someone by your words or deeds? Have you stolen, been negligent, wasted anything, or done any harm?

What is the Office of the Keys?

The Office of the Keys is that special authority which Christ has given to His church on earth to forgive the sins of repentant sinners, but to withhold forgiveness from the unrepentant as long as they do not repent.

Where is this written?

This is what St. John the Evangelist writes in chapter twenty: The Lord Jesus breathed on His disciples and said, "Receive the Holy Spirit. If you forgive anyone his sins, they are forgiven; if you do not forgive them, they are not forgiven." *[John 20:22–23]*

What do you believe according to these words?

I believe that when the called ministers of Christ deal with us by His divine command, in particular when they exclude openly unrepentant sinners from the Christian congregation and absolve those who repent of their sins and want to do better, this is just as valid and certain, even in heaven, as if Christ our dear Lord dealt with us Himself.

As the head of the family should teach it in a simple way to his household

> The church can live through the delay
> of Christ's return [the parousia], for in
> every celebration of the Lord's Supper
> a parousia already occurs. We are the
> people of God wandering through the
> wilderness of this world, preserved by
> the spiritual food and drink of the
> Lord's Supper."
>
> —Hermann Sasse[51]

What is the Sacrament of the Altar?

It is the true body and blood of our Lord Jesus Christ under the bread and wine, instituted by Christ Himself for us Christians to eat and to drink.

Where is this written?

The holy Evangelists Matthew, Mark, Luke, and St. Paul write:

Our Lord Jesus Christ, on the night when He was betrayed, took bread, and when He had

given thanks, He broke it and gave it to the disciples and said: "Take, eat; this is My body, which is given for you. This do in remembrance of Me."

In the same way also He took the cup after supper, and when He had given thanks, He gave it to them, saying, "Drink of it, all of you; this cup is the new testament in My blood, which is shed for you for the forgiveness of sins. This do, as often as you drink it, in remembrance of Me."

What is the benefit of this eating and drinking?

These words, "Given and shed for you for the forgiveness of sins," show us that in the Sacrament forgiveness of sins, life, and salvation are given us through these words. For where there is forgiveness of sins, there is also life and salvation.

How can bodily eating and drinking do such great things?

Certainly not just eating and drinking do these things, but the words written here: "Given and shed for you for the forgiveness of sins." These words, along with the bodily eating and drinking, are the main thing in the Sacrament. Whoever believes these words has exactly what they say: "forgiveness of sins."

Who receives this sacrament worthily?

Fasting and bodily preparation are certainly fine outward training. But that person is truly worthy and well prepared who has faith in these words: "Given and shed for you for the forgiveness of sins."

But anyone who does not believe these words or doubts them is unworthy and unprepared, for the words "for you" require all hearts to believe.

How the head of the family should teach his household to pray morning and evening

Morning Prayer—

In the morning when you get up, make the sign of the holy cross and say:

In the name of the Father and of the ✠ Son and of the Holy Spirit. Amen.

Then, kneeling or standing, repeat the Creed and the Lord's Prayer. If you choose, you may also say this little prayer:

I thank You, my heavenly Father, through Jesus Christ, Your dear Son, that You have kept me this night from all harm and danger; and I pray that You would keep me this day also from sin and every evil, that all my doings and life may please You. For into Your hands I commend myself, my body and soul, and all things. Let Your holy angel be with me, that the evil foe may have no power over me. Amen.

Then go joyfully to your work, singing a hymn, like that of the Ten Commandments, or whatever your devotion may suggest.

Evening Prayer—

In the evening when you go to bed, make the sign of the holy cross and say:

In the name of the Father and of the ✙ Son and of the Holy Spirit. Amen.

Then kneeling or standing, repeat the Creed and the Lord's Prayer. If you choose, you may also say this little prayer:

I thank You, my heavenly Father, through Jesus Christ, Your dear Son, that You have graciously kept me this day; and I pray that You would forgive me all my sins where I have done wrong, and graciously keep me this night. For into Your hands I commend myself, my body and soul, and all things. Let Your holy angel be with me, that the evil foe may have no power over me. Amen.

Then go to sleep at once and in good cheer.

How the head of the family should teach his household to ask a blessing and return thanks

Asking a Blessing—

The children and the members of the household shall go to the table reverently, fold their hands, and say:

The eyes of all look to You, O Lord, and You give them their food at the proper time. You open your hand and satisfy the desires of every living thing. [Psalm 145:15–16]

Then shall be said the Lord's Prayer and the following:

Lord God, heavenly Father, bless us and these Your gifts which we receive from Your bountiful goodness, through Jesus Christ, our Lord. Amen.

Returning Thanks—

Also, after eating, they shall, in like manner, reverently and with folded hands say:

Give thanks to the Lord, for He is good, His love endures forever. He gives food to every creature. He provides food for the cattle and for the young ravens when they call. His pleasure is not in the strength of the horse, nor His delight in the legs of a man; the Lord delights in those who fear Him, who put their hope in His unfailing love. [Psalm 136:1, 25; 147:9–11]

Then shall be said the Lord's Prayer and the following:

We thank You, Lord God, heavenly Father, for all Your benefits, through Jesus Christ, our Lord, who lives and reigns with You and the Holy Spirit forever and ever. Amen.

Certain passages of Scripture for various holy orders and positions, admonishing them about their duties and responsibilities

To Bishops, Pastors, and Preachers—

The overseer must be above reproach, the husband of but one wife, temperate, self-controlled, respectable, hospitable, able to teach, not given to drunkenness, not violent but gentle, not quarrelsome, not a lover of money. He must manage his own family well and see that his children obey him with proper respect. *1 Timothy 3:2–4*

He must not be a recent convert, or he may become conceited and fall under the same judgment as the devil. *1 Timothy 3:6*

He must hold firmly to the trustworthy message as it has been taught, so that he can encourage others by sound doctrine and refute those who oppose it. *Titus 1:9*

What the Hearers Owe Their Pastors—

The Lord has commanded that those who preach the Gospel should receive their living from the Gospel. *1 Corinthians 9:14*

Anyone who receives instruction in the Word

must share all good things with his instructor. Do not be deceived: God cannot be mocked. A man reaps what he sows. *Galatians 6:6–7*

The elders who direct the affairs of the church well are worthy of double honor, especially those whose work is preaching and teaching. For the Scripture says, "Do not muzzle the ox while it is treading out the grain," and "The worker deserves his wages." *1 Timothy 5:17–18*

We ask you, brothers, to respect those who work hard among you, who are over you in the Lord and who admonish you. Hold them in the highest regard in love because of their work. Live in peace with each other. *1 Thessalonians 5:12–13*

Obey your leaders and submit to their authority. They keep watch over you as men who must give an account. Obey them so that their work will be a joy, not a burden, for that would be of no advantage to you. *Hebrews 13:17*

Of Civil Government—

Everyone must submit himself to the governing authorities, for there is no authority except that which God has established. The authorities that exist have been established by God. Consequently, he who rebels against the authority is rebelling against what God has instituted, and those who do so will bring judgment on themselves. For rulers hold no terror for those who do right, but for those who do wrong. Do you want to be free from fear of the one in authority? Then do what is right and he will commend you. For he is God's servant to do you good. But if you do wrong, be afraid, for he does not bear the sword for nothing. He is God's servant, an agent of wrath to bring punishment on the wrongdoer. *Romans 13:1–4*

Of Citizens—

Give to Caesar what is Caesar's, and to God what is God's. *Matthew 22:21*

It is necessary to submit to the authorities, not only because of possible punishment but also because of conscience. This is also why you pay taxes, for the authorities are God's servants, who give their full time to governing. Give everyone what you owe him: If you owe taxes, pay taxes; if revenue, then revenue; if respect, then respect; if honor, then honor. *Romans 13:5–7*

I urge, then, first of all, that requests, prayers, intercession and thanksgiving be made for everyone—for kings and all those in authority, that we may live peaceful and quiet lives in all godliness and holiness. This is good, and pleases God our Savior. *1 Timothy 2:1–3*

Remind the people to be subject to rulers and authorities, to be obedient, to be ready to do whatever is good. *Titus 3:1*

Submit yourselves for the Lord's sake to every authority instituted among men: whether to the king, as the supreme authority, or to governors, who are sent by him to punish those who do wrong and to commend those who do right. *1 Peter 2:13–14*

To Husbands—

Husbands, in the same way be considerate as you live with your wives, and treat them with respect as the weaker partner and as heirs with you of the gracious gift of life, so that nothing will hinder your prayers. *1 Peter 3:7*

Husbands, love your wives and do not be harsh with them. *Colossians 3:19*

To Wives—

Wives, submit to your husbands as to the Lord. *Ephesians 5:22*

They were submissive to their own husbands, like Sarah, who obeyed Abraham and called him her master. You are her daughters if you do what is right and do not give way to fear. *1 Peter 3:5–6*

To Parents—

Fathers, do not exasperate your children; instead, bring them up in the training and instruction of the Lord. *Ephesians 6:4*

To Children—

Children, obey your parents in the Lord, for this is right. "Honor your father and your mother"—which is the first commandment with a promise—"that it may go well with you and that you may enjoy long life on the earth." *Ephesians 6:1–3*

To Workers of All Kinds—

Slaves, obey your earthly masters with respect and fear, and with sincerity of heart, just as you would obey Christ. Obey them not only to win their favor when their eye is on you, but like slaves of Christ, doing the will of God from your heart. Serve wholeheartedly, as if you were serving the Lord, not men, because you know that the Lord will reward everyone for whatever good he does, whether he is slave or free. *Ephesians 6:5–8*

To Employers and Supervisors—

Masters, treat your slaves in the same way. Do not threaten them, since you know that he who is both their Master and yours is in heaven, and there is no favoritism with Him. *Ephesians 6:9*

To Youth—

Young men, in the same way be submissive to those who are older. All of you clothe yourselves with humility toward one another, because, "God opposes the proud but gives grace to the humble." Humble yourselves, therefore, under God's mighty hand, that He may lift you up in due time. *1 Peter 5:5–6*

To Widows—

The widow who is really in need and left all alone puts her hope in God and continues night and day to pray and to ask God for help. But the widow who lives for pleasure is dead even while she lives. *1 Timothy 5:5–6*

To Everyone—

The commandments . . . are summed up in this one rule: "Love your neighbor as yourself." *Romans 13:9*

I urge . . . that requests, prayers, intercession and thanksgiving be made for everyone. *1 Timothy 2:1*

Let each his lesson learn with care,
And all the household well shall fare.

Reader's Guide
to Scripture's Essential Teachings

These references are presented to encourage the study of, and the meditation on, the essential teachings of Scripture. This is by no means an exhaustive list, nor are all the great topics of Scripture and doctrine listed. In addition to inclusion in personal devotions these references can serve as an outline for discussion or confession of the faith.

Creation and the Doctrine of Man
  Genesis 1–2
  Job 10:8–12; 38:8–9, 19–20
  Genesis 3

Justification by Grace through Faith
  Ephesians 2:16; Romans 8:6–8
  Romans 3:23–24
  2 Corinthians 5:21
  Romans 4:25
  1 Corinthians 15:20–23
  1 Peter 1:3–4
  John 3:17–18
  Ephesians 2:8–9
  Romans 6:3–4; 8:1–4

Sanctification
  Philippians 4:4,8
  Romans 8:2–11

One God in Three Persons
  Isaiah 44:6
  Deuteronomy 4:35; 6:4–19
  1 Corinthians 8:6
  Genesis 1:26

Baptism of Jesus;
Transfiguration of Jesus
  John 14:9–10
  Matthew 28:19
  Ephesians 2:18
  1 John 4:13
  1 Corinthians 12:3
  2 Corinthians 3:18

The Nature of God
  Psalm 40:11; 51:1; 54:1; 85:7
  Psalm 10:15; 59:5; 80:4
  Psalm 53:2–3, 5
  John 3:16

The Nature of God, *cont.*
Psalm 85:4–7
Psalm 86:15
Romans 1:16–17
1 John 4:8–10

Jesus Christ: The God Man
John 1:1–4,14,16
Luke 2:1–20
Hebrews 2:14–18; 4:15
1 Peter 2:22–24; 3:18

The Means of Grace
2 Corinthians 5:19
Romans 3:21–28
Romans 1:16
Matthew 28:19
Ephesians 5:26
Titus 3:3–6
Romans 6:3–10

The Means of Grace, *cont.*
Colossians 2:12–13
1 Corinthians 12:12–13
Matthew 26:26–29
Mark 14:22–25
Luke 22:15–20
1 Corinthians 10:14–22;
11:17–34
Revelation 19:7–9

The Church of Jesus Christ
2 Timothy 1:9
Ephesians 1:18; 4:11
Colossians 1:12–20
1 Corinthians 6:11
Galatians 3:26–29
1 Peter 2:9–10
Hebrews 10:25
Ephesians 4:1–16
Ephesians 2:20

If a person but opens his eyes he will find among us many saints, not identified by monk's clothing, but hidden in the habit of daily life. May God give us many of our saints and grant that we may see their splendor on that day when it really matters!
—Loehe[52]

Let us therefore walk as if we were on the way; for the king of our homeland has made Himself the way to it . . . There He is the truth; here, the way. Where do we go? To truth. How do we go? By faith. Where do we go? To Christ. How do we go? Through Christ.

—Augustine[53]

Suggestions for a Contemporary Christian's Library

Bible
Hymnal

Confessions of the Evangelical Church

Luther's Small Catechism with Explanation. Saint Louis: Concordia Publishing House, (1986) 1999.

Concordia: The Faith of the Christian Church (The Book of Concord, including Bente's Historical Introduction), edited by Paul McCain, Ed Engelbrecht, Robert Baker, and Gene Edward Vieth. Saint Louis: Concordia Publishing House, 2005.

Getting into the Theology of Concord, Robert D. Preus. Saint Louis: Concordia Publishing House, 1998.

Summary of Christian Doctrine, Edward Koehler; revised by A. Koehler. Saint Louis: Concordia Publishing House, 2005.

To All Eternity: The Essential Teachings of Christianity, edited by Edward Engelbrecht. St. Louis: Concordia Publishing House, 2001.

> The sages, it is often said, can see no
> answer to the riddle of religion.
> But the trouble with our sages is not
> that they cannot see the answer; it is
> that they cannot even see the riddle...
> The modern critics of religious authority
> are like men who should attack the police
> without ever having heard of burglars.
> —G. K. Chesterton[5]

> Faith is the mother of all worldly
> energies, but its foes are the fathers
> of all worldly confusion. The secular-
> ists have not wrecked a divine thing;
> but the secularists have wrecked a
> secular thing, if that is any comfort to
> them. The Titans did not scale heav'n;
> but they laid waste the world.
> —G. K. Chesterton[55]

Martin Luther

Luther: Biography of a Reformer, Frederick Nohl. Saint Louis:
Concordia Publishing House, 2003.

Luther the Reformer: The Story of the Man and His Career, James
Kittelson. Minneapolis: Augsburg Fortress, 2003.

Luther's Prayers, edited by Herbert Brokering. Minneapolis:
Augsburg Fortress, 1994.

How to Live A Christian Life, Martin Luther; adapted by Paul
Strawn. Minneapolis: Lutheran Press, 2003.

*On Being a Theologian of the Cross: Reflections on Luther's
Heidelberg Disputation*, 1518, Gerhard O. Forde. Grand Rapids:
Eerdmanns, 1997.

The 1529 Holy Week and Easter Sermons of Dr. Martin Luther,
translated by Irving L. Sandberg. St. Louis: Concordia
Academic Press, 1999.

Faith and Life

Dying to Live: The Power of Forgiveness, Harold Senkbeil. Saint
Louis: Concordia Publishing House, 1994.

Hammer of God, Bo Giertz. Minneapolis: Augsburg Fortress, 1960.

Handling the Word of Truth: Law and Gospel in the Church Today.
Saint Louis: Concordia Publishing House, 2005.

God at Work: Your Christian Vocation in All of Life, Gene Edward
Vieth, Jr. Wheaton, Illinois: Crossway Books, April 1, 2002.

Faith and Life, *cont.*

God's No and God's Yes, C. F. W. Walther. Saint Louis: Concordia Publishing House, 1973.

Life Together, Dietrich Bonhoeffer. San Francisco: HarperSanFrancisco, 1978.

Mere Christianity, C.S. Lewis. San Francisco: Harper Collins Publishers, 2001.

On Becoming a Christian, Henry Hamann, Appleton, Wisconsin: Northwestern Publishing House, 1996.

The Defense Never Rests: A Lawyer's Quest for the Gospel, Craig Parton. Saint Louis: Concordia Publishing House, 2003.

The Fire and the Staff: Pure Doctrine and Pastoral Ministry, Klemet Preus. Saint Louis: Concordia Publishing House, 2005.

The Lord's Prayer, Martin Chemnitz. Saint Louis: Concordia Publishing House, 1999.

The Spirituality of the Cross, Gene Edward Vieth. Saint Louis: Concordia Publishing House, 1999.

The Quest for Holiness, Adolf Koberle. Minneapolis: Augsburg, 1936.

We Confess Series. Hermann Sasse, translated by Norman Nagel. St. Louis: Concordia Publishing House, 1984.

Where in the World is God. Harold L. Senkbeil. Appleton, Wisconsin: Northwestern Publishing House, 1999.

Why I am a Lutheran, Daniel Preus. Saint Louis: Concordia Publishing House, 2004.

Devotional Materials

Lutheran Book of Prayer, edited by Scot Kinnaman. St. Louis: Concordia Publishing House, 2005.

Meditations on Divine Mercy: A Classic Treasury of Devotional Prayers, Johann Gerhard, translated by Matthew Harrison. St. Louis: Concordia Publishing House, 2003.

The Lord Will Answer: A Daily Prayer Catechism, edited by Edward Engelbrecht. St. Louis: Concordia Publishing House, 2004.

Through Faith Alone: 365 Devotional Readings from Martin Luther, edited by James C. Galvin, St. Louis: Concordia Publishing House, 1999.

The royal banners forward go.
This is a not a parade that
we may watch. The banners
summon us, God's sons and
daughters, God's workers,
God's guests. We have the
fearful freedom, the freedom
to evade, to rebel, to despise.
But no; we do not really have it.
The Son has set us free from
that fatal freedom; He has
set us free for God.

—Martin Franzmann[53]

He who knows what compelling
reason God has for judging him,
will begin to listen in a fresh
manner of the Savior who does
not judge—not because Jesus
needs forgiveness and not
because he had no occasion to
judge, but because he has taken
upon Himself His brothers'
destiny and has died in the
place of sinners.

—Bo Giertz[56]

Notes

1. Korby, Kenneth F., "Prayer: Pre-Reformation to the Present," in *Christians at Prayer,* ed. John Gallen (Notre Dame, Indiana: University of Notre Dame Press, 1977), 113-116.

2. Bonhoeffer, Dietrich, *Psalms: The Prayer Book of the Bible* (Minneapolis: Augsburg Fortress, 1970), 46.

3. Pless, John T. *Prayer: The Voice of God,* an academic paper published on the website of Concordia Theological Seminary, Fort Wayne (http://www.ctsfw.edu/academics/faculty/pless/prayer.htm), used by permission of Concordia Theological Seminary.

4. *Luther's Small Catechism,* The Lord's Prayer (Saint. Louis: Concordia, 1989), 17.

5. Bonhoeffer, *Psalms* 15.

6. Walther, C. F. W., *The Proper Distinction Between Law and Gospel* (Saint Louis: Concordia, 1928), 2.

7. Peterson, Eugene, *Answering God: The Psalms as Tools for Prayer* (New York: Harper and Row, 1989), 15.

8. Koberle, Adolf, *The Quest For Holiness: A Biblical, Historical And Systematic Investigation* (Minneapolis: Augsburg, 1938), 176–177.

9. *Tractatus in evangelium Ioannis 2.2,* trans. John Rettig, *The Fathers of the Church,* Volume 78 (Washington D.C.: Catholic University of America), 62.

10. Chesterton, G.K., *Orthodoxy* (New York: The John Lane Company, 1908), 235.

11. Senkbeil, Harold L., *Triumph of the Cross* (Milwaukee: Northwestern, 1999), 132.

12. Goerss, Ronald, "Fashion me in Your image," in *Meditations for College Students* (Saint Louis: Concordia, 1961), 91, 92.

13. Loehe, Wilhelm, *Three Books about the Church,* trans. James Schaaf (Philadelphia: Fortress, 1969), 50.

14. Augustine, *Confessions* Book I, I (1), translated with Introduction and Notes by Henry Chadwick (Oxford University Press, 1991), 3.

15. Hamann, Henry, *On Being a Christian* (Milwaukee: Northwestern, 1996), 58.

16. Augustine, *Enarationes in psalmos* 127.3, in *Augustine and The Catechumenate*, by William Harmless [translation here by Harmless] (Collegeville, Minnesota: Liturgical Press, 1995), 212.

17. Chesterton, G. K., *The Everlasting Man* (San Francisco: Ignatius Press, 1993), 213.

18. Sasse, Hermann, *We Confess*, Part III (Saint Louis: Concordia, 1999), 136.

19. Lewis, C. S., "Religion: Reality or Substitute," in *Christian Reflections* (Grand Rapids: Eerdmans, 1967), 44.

20. The Large Catechism in *The Book of Concord: The Confessions of the Evangelical Lutheran Church*, ed. Theodore G. Tappert (Philadelphia: Fortress Press, 1959), 1, 2–3; 28.

21. Goerss, *Meditations*, 95, 96.

22. Chesterton, *Othodoxy*, 85.

23. Sasse, *We Confess*, 132.

24. Koberle, *Quest for Holiness*, 246.

25. Goerss, *Meditations*, 97, 98.

26. Senkbeil, Harold L., *Where in the World Is God?* (Milwaukee: Northwestern, 1999), 64.

27. Franzmann, Martin, *Ha! Ha! Among the Trumpets. Sermons by Martin Franzmann* (St. Louis: Concordia, 1999), 63.

28. Goerss, *Meditations*, 99, 100.

29. Sasse, *We Confess*, 25.

30. Senkbeil, *Where in the World*, 51.

31. Koberle, *Quest*, 243.

32. Sasse, Hermann, "Flight from Dogma," in *The Lonely Way* vol. 2 (St. Louis: Concordia, 2002), 113.

33. Goerss, *Meditations*, 103, 104.

34. Loehe, *Three Books*, 148.

35. Senkbeil, Harold L., *Dying to Live* (St. Louis: Concordia, 1994), 145.

36. Senkbeil, *Dying to Live*, 147.

37. Koberle, *Quest*, 123.

38. Loehe, *Three Books*, 148.

39. Wessling, Edward W., "A Student Speaks On...: A Collection of Student-composed Meditations," in *Meditations for College Students* (Saint Louis: Concordia, 1961), 147, 148.
40. Giertz, Bo, *Preaching from the Whole Bible*, trans. Clifford Nelson (Minneapolis: Augsburg, 1967), 109.
41. Sasse, *Flight from Dogma*, 116.
42. Senkbeil, *Triumph*, 136.
43. Koberle, *Quest*, 116.
44. Goerrs, *Meditations*, 109.
45. Giertz, *Preaching*, 69.
46. Hamann, *Being Christian*, 64.
47. Lewis, *Christian Reflections*, 43.
48. Sasse, *Dogma*, 106.
49. Koberle, *Quest*, 253.
50. Sasse, Hermann, "Circular Letter 4 to Westphalian Pastors—On Baptism," *The Lonely Way* vol. 2 (St. Louis: Concordia, 2002), 159.
51. Sasse, *We Confess*, 132.
52. Loehe, *Three Books*, 145.
53. Franzmann, *Ha! Ha!*, 63.
54. Chesterton, *Orthodoxy*, 260.
55. Hamann, *Being a Christian*, 81.
56. Giertz, *Preaching*, 79.

> Hope for the future, for death and the beyond, fits the Christian even better for this life, for love for his neighbor, and for the task of taking the Gospel to all people, so that they too may be brought to salvation."
> —Henry Hamann[55]

1 2 3 4 5 6 7 8 9 10   14 13 12 11 10 09 08 07 06 05